Design, Technology and the Development Process in the Built Environment

THE BUILT ENVIRONMENT SERIES OF TEXTBOOKS (BEST)

Executive Editor:	Professor Tony Collier, Dean, Faculty of the Built Environment, University of Central England, Birmingham, UK
Co-ordinating Editor:	David Burns, Faculty of the Built Environment, University of Central England, Birmingham, UK
Assistant Editor:	Jean Bacon, Faculty of the Built Environment, University of Central England, Birmingham, UK

ADVISORY BOARD:

James Armstrong *Visiting Professor, Faculty of Technology, Kingston University*

David Cormican *Deputy Director, North West Institute of Further and Higher Education*

Bryan Jefferson *Architectural Advisor to the Secretary of State, Department of National Heritage.*
Visiting Professor, Sheffield University, Faculty of Architectural Studies

Howard Land *Professional Training Consultant, RICS*

Alan Osborne *Chairman, Tarmac Construction Ltd*
Chairman, Construction Industry Standing Conference (CISC)

John Tarn *Roscoe Professor of Architecture, University of Liverpool*

Alan Wenban-Smith *Assistant Director of Planning and Architecture, Birmingham City Council*

This series of textbooks responds to changes that are occurring throughout the construction industry and in higher and further education. It focuses on aspects of the curriculum that are common to all professions in the built environment. The principal aim of BEST is to provide texts that are relevant to more than one course and the texts therefore address areas of commonality in an original and innovative way. Learning aids in the texts such as chapter objectives, checklists, and workpieces will appeal to all students.

OTHER TITLES IN THE SERIES:

Collaborative Practice in the Built Environment
Business Skills in the Built Environment

Forthcoming
Law and the Built Environment
Buildings, Neighbourhoods and Places
Environmental Issues in the Built Environment
International Trends in the Construction Industry
Economics and the Built Environment
Management and Business Skills in the Built Environment

DESIGN, TECHNOLOGY AND THE DEVELOPMENT PROCESS IN THE BUILT ENVIRONMENT

EDITED BY TONY COLLIER

Faculty of the Built Environment, University of
Central England, Birmingham, UK

E & FN SPON
An Imprint of Chapman & Hall

London · Glasgow · Weinheim · New York · Tokyo · Melbourne · Madras

**Published by E & FN Spon, an imprint of Chapman & Hall,
2–6 Boundary Row, London SE1 8HN, UK**

Chapman & Hall, 2–6 Boundary Row, London SE1 8HN, UK

Blackie Academic & Professional, Wester Cleddens Road, Bishopbriggs,
Glasgow G64 2NZ, UK

Chapman & Hall GmbH, Pappelallee 3, 69469 Weinheim, Germany

Chapman & Hall USA, 115 Fifth Avenue, New York NY 10003, USA

Chapman & Hall Japan, ITP-Japan, Kyowa Building, 3F, 2-21 Hirakawacho,
Chiyoda-ku, Tokyo 102, Japan

Chapman & Hall Australia, Thomas Nelson Australia, 102 Dodds Street,
South Melbourne, Victoria 3205, Australia

Chapman & Hall India, R. Seshadri, 32 Second Main Road, CIT East, Madras
600 035, India

First edition 1995

© 1995 E & FN Spon

Typeset in 10/12pt Caslon by Saxon Graphics Ltd, Derby

Printed in Great Britain by the Alden Press, Osney Mead, Oxford

ISBN 0 419 19550 5

A catalogue record for this book is available from the British Library

Library of Congress Catalog Card Number: 94-74711

∞ Printed on permanent acid-free text paper, manufactured in accordance
with ANSI/NISO Z39.48-1992 and ANSI/NISO Z39.48-1984 (Permanence of
Paper).

CONTENTS

CONTRIBUTORS

Jean Badman
Head of School of Estate
    Management
University of Central England
Birmingham

David Boyd
Principal Lecturer, School of
    Architecture
University of Central England
Birmingham

Ann Burns
Marketing Executive
Wimpey Homes
Wimpey plc

David Chapman
Head of School Planning
University of Central England
Birmingham

Tony Collier
Dean of Faculty of the Built
    Environment
University of Central England
Birmingham

Robert Grimshaw
Head of School of Building and
    Building Surveying
University of Central England
Birmingham

Alan Middleton
Associate Dean of Faculty of the
    Built Environment
University of Central England
Birmingham

Adrian Napper
Head of School of Architecture
Heriot Watt University
Edinburgh

Robert Templeton
Senior Lecturer, School of
    Building and Building Surveying
University of Central England
Birmingham

Arthur Yarnell
Senior Lecturer, School of
    Building and Building Surveying
University of Central England
Birmingham

ACKNOWLEDGMENTS

Figures have been supplied by kind permission of the following:

Richard Andrews: Figure 10.3

Alastair Carew-Cox: Figure 2.4

David Chapman: Figures 4.1, 4.3, 6.3

Tony Collier: Figures 2.2, 7.4, 7.5, 10.4, 10.5

Peter Maddern: Figures 5.1, 6.1

Alan Middleton: Figure 2.3

Mission Aviation Fellowship UK: Figure 2.1

Tom Muir: Figures 1.1, 1.2, 1.3, 1.4, 3.1, 3.2, 4.4, 5.2, 5.3, 6.1, 6.2, 10.1, 10.2.

Steve Roddie: Figure 4.2

INTRODUCTION

This book explores the fundamental generators and contextual issues – philosophical, physical and political – that influence the built environment. It draws on international examples to show how societies and cultures in different parts of the world react to similar problems. It contrasts dramatically different types of buildings and enclosures from primitive shelters to the lunar module to show how humans endeavour to control the environment – wherever it is.

Interwoven into the book are four underlying themes:

- Social, political and economic forces which shape our towns and cities and the way people have interacted in the creation of buildings and places.
- How society and technology are changing and the way these changes impact on the environment.
- How humans intervene with nature, in particular in the control of climate and the provision of protected space through the use of structure, the building skin and services.
- The nature of problem solving activities in the development of the built environment, in particular in the design of buildings.

The book addresses issues that all young built environment professionals need to know regardless of their future career specialisms. It is aimed primarily at first year undergraduate students on built environment courses. Depending on the structure of courses it may well also be relevant to students in later years of their degrees as well as to pre-qualification education and training in some B.Tec or general environmental courses.

Consequently, this book is about the integration of design, technology and the development process. It is about the elements that make up buildings and the ideas that generate them. It is also about the nature and availability of materials, structural and spatial concepts and the impact of social order and political goals on the built environment. Fundamental relationships and principles are explored in their cultural and economic context. Radically different buildings and structures are

ABOUT THIS BOOK

identified and compared. Issues and problems common to all buildings are revealed.

Throughout history people have intervened in the environment. Who knows what was the earliest intervention or the reasons for it? If we look at any period from prehistoric times, ancient Greece and Rome to the Middle Ages and the twentieth century, we can examine the way individuals and societies have intervened in the environment and their relative success in this. Such examination can also establish the purposes of intervention – for example to create better conditions for survival and a pleasanter 'life style'.

The book has three broad objectives:

- To explore the relationships between design, technology and the development process in the context of society as a whole and to understand their interaction as a creative force.
- To identify a framework to assist in the analysis of buildings as technological, design and cultural achievements.
- To trace, through a variety of building types in different periods and cultures, the way problems were solved by identifying problems or issues common to a range of buildings.

STRUCTURE

The structure of the book, which is in three parts, is important to understand. Part One comprises Chapters 1–3 and is about the fundamental challenges that have confronted built environment professionals today and in the past. The first three chapters use a rich and diverse range of examples from many different countries, cultures and periods. Chapter 1 sets the scene by exploring generations of buildings and contrasting well known types of architecture and structures to illustrate basic ideas and needs that influence all buildings. Chapter 2 presents the social challenge – the fundamental forces which influence the way society has developed the environment and constructed buildings. In Chapter 3 we are challenged about the way we think about and use technology in relation to the design and development process. It links scientific and technological change with social change.

Part Two discusses the nature of the development of buildings, villages, towns and cities and their construction. It commences with Chapter 4 which discusses the nature of 'place', how groups of buildings have evolved and the way we define the quality and character of what we like. The approach shifts in Chapter 5 to an analysis of the development process itself, the way places have evolved and the nature of the development process today. Chapter 6 picks up these threads in a historical context and illustrates the way design is influenced by technical innovation and contemporary thinking. This chapter bridges with Parts Two and Three.

Part Three is very much about the nature of structure and the construction of buildings. Chapter 7 is called 'Concepts of structure and space' and deals with the essence of structure, using the human body as an analogy. In Chapter 8 we explore the nature of the building skin, i.e. the clothes that go on a structure to form the space inside. Chapter 9 explains the why and how of services – the basics of heating, lighting and other services like lifts and air-conditioning in buildings.

The final chapter draws together these strands with particular reference to the breadth of problem solving activities in the built environment, especially those to do with design and the future of the design, development and construction team.

While all the chapters connect and are grouped into these three parts, each can also be read as a chapter in its own right. Because of the diverse range of material and the way the book promotes an understanding of the whole design, development process and technological impact of buildings, it has been written by a range of specialist authors. All the authors have used the same format so that while style may vary each chapter is organized into a common format and includes theme and objectives, introduction, summary, checklist, workpieces, references and further reading. The workpieces have been carefully thought out to enable students and teachers to benefit from either individual or group learning using common material. Most of the workpieces are designed to encourage discussion and develop skills in critical analysis as well as promote the individual knowledge base of each reader and establish a spirit of enquiry in each reader.

CHAPTER SUMMARIES
PART ONE
THE FUNDAMENTAL
CHALLENGES

CHAPTER 1 VISION AND INTERVENTION

The opening chapter is about the nature of intervention; people, comfort, climate. It sets a historical perspective about vision and design and the way we intervene with nature, using practical examples of buildings and structures from all around the world including the Gothic cathedral, lunar module and a French garden.

CHAPTER 2 THE SOCIAL CHALLENGE

What are the social generators of the built environment? The movement of people, social order; cultural impacts and social change; the user and client in the broader context. The development process – its context in the control or use of land for building, including governmental policies and the relationship between global issues and regional strategies.

CHAPTER 3 THE CHALLENGE OF TECHNOLOGY

The extraordinary pace of technological change has and will continue to be a major issue for society. How does such change impact on the built environment and on society? The connections are illustrated through a potted history of technology; the use of Technology Assessment methods, innovations and inventions such as lifts, services, air-conditioning and computer aided design.

PART TWO

THE PROCESS OF

DEVELOPMENT –

CREATING A SENSE OF

PLACE

CHAPTER 4 BUILDING TOGETHER

Are there fundamental principles which influence the way people relate to each other and to the land? How do they influence the way buildings and spaces relate to each other? Environmental factors, cultural values and human aspirations are discussed in relation to creating a sense of place,and the ways to study places to assess their quality and how they might be improved.

CHAPTER 5 UK DEVELOPMENT PROCESSES IN AN INTERNATIONAL CONTEXT

Whatever our role in the environment, it is essential to understand the nature of the development process as a whole and the ideas and legislation behind it. Topics include the role of the team, the basis of UK planning law, the impact of EU legislation and other international comparisons.

CHAPTER 6 BUILDING IN A CONTEXT

Traditionally building methods related closely to the local economy and the availability of materials. Buildings can be dated and located in clear geographical and historical contexts. This chapter, a linking chapter between Parts Two and Three, emphasizes the historical perspective – in particular the evolution of Roman architecture. It explores relationships between constructional materials and techniques and the building of structures as well as government control on building and political ideology.

PART THREE

THE DESIGN AND

CONSTRUCTION OF

BUILDINGS

CHAPTER 7 CONCEPTS OF STRUCTURE AND SPACE

Without structure, buildings collapse. All built environment professionals should therefore have an understanding of the fundamental principles of structure and their relative impact. Structural systems are explained (using the human body as an analogy) as is their relationship to approaches to design and development, including historical and modern examples of uses of structural materials and types.

CHAPTER 8 THE BUILDING SKIN

The key determinant in modifying climate and the visual appearance of buildings is the nature of the building 'skin'. The use and expression in different countries and cultures, from igloo and mud hut to vernacular architecture in the UK and the modern building, is explored. A detailed analysis of performance needs of the building skin is given.

CHAPTER 9 ASPECTS OF ENGINEERING SERVICES IN DESIGN AND DEVELOPMENT

The incorporation of services within buildings is necessary for the provision of a safe, comfortable and convenient environment. This chapter evaluates the nature and use of services and their impact on comfort, from plumbing and ducted warm air in Roman villas to contemporary 'hightech' buildings, including the relationships between the design and installation of services and the overall design of a building.

CHAPTER 10 INDIVIDUAL AND COLLECTIVE RESPONSIBILITIES

The final chapter draws together the strands set out in the book as a whole in a discussion about the nature of change and future challenges. It relates the book to others in the series and sets the context for further enquiry.

PART ONE

THE FUNDAMENTAL CHALLENGES

VISION AND INTERVENTION

TONY COLLIER

THEME

However far back in history we look, people have always found ways to improve their physical conditions through the creation of shelter and enclosures. Animals seek shelter in poor weather. The idea of shelter is fundamental to any society but so is the desire to embellish and decorate buildings, giving expression to spiritual needs. Using a diverse array of examples such as a cave dwelling, a lunar module and a Gothic cathedral, this chapter explores issues and problems which are common to buildings, whatever the context, and establishes a framework for analysing them.

OBJECTIVES

After reading this chapter you should be able to:

● identify and distinguish between generators of buildings;

● identify a range of environmental conditions which build-ings must modify to achieve comfort;

● understand cultural, social, political and economic con-straints which have affected buildings through the ages;

● understand the concepts and information contained in this book.

INTRODUCTION

This chapter takes an overview of the book as a whole and looks at some of the questions for which technology is the answer. If technology is to be utilized well, questions need to be asked and their implications understood. Here we will be identifying and exploring some of these

3

questions. But are they questions about creating comfort, cultural expression or the way society is organized?

Intervention is about problem solving. In order to solve problems we need to ask questions, analyse and find solutions. The successful analysis of a problem will depend on having a critical framework. This book is about both evolving a set of questions and achieving a series of outcomes. It is student centred and requires a significant element of self-awareness and motivation. It aims to assist students in establishing their own critical framework.

Let us look at the simplest and most basic forms of shelter we can think of, such as a sheep pen and a cave dwelling. Both provide the most primitive forms of enclosure. One is for animals; for example, sheep exposed to driving rain, wind, ice and snow on wild moorlands and open countryside will huddle together in these pens, which can be seen today. The other in its most primitive form gave prehistoric people a degree of security and protection from wild animals as well as the weather. A cave dwelling may not be the most attractive of places by today's standards but in prehistoric times it was better than no protection at all.

Art crept into buildings in surprisingly early times. Much has been written about cave paintings. Are these decorated caves the earliest form of architecture? Why did prehistoric man need to decorate caves

Figure 1.1 Primitive community shelter assumed to be about 700–900BC, Skara Brae in the Orkneys, Scotland. (Tom Muir.)

Figure 1.2   Cave-painting: decoration by prehistoric man. (Tom Muir.)

with paintings? Was the representation of animals like the mammoth on cave walls some sort of symbolism to do with hunting? Historians have had difficulty defining and placing prehistoric art – its date, purposes and traditions.

Even taking such early and basic examples of a dwelling raises questions about art and culture, social organization and performance.

How well does the cave perform as a shelter and for security?

WORKPIECE 1.1

SHELTER AND SECURITY

Security and shelter can be provided in many ways. On a camping holiday people are content to have simple shelter and limited security. In some parts of the world people live in what we might call primitive conditions, yet their quality of life may be high. Minimum standards for a UK citizen may be very different from those of a developing country.

Identify three different types of shelter used today in three different climates (three regions of a particular country or three different countries), e.g. igloo, terrace house in UK, high-rise flat in Hong Kong.

List the climatic conditions for each place.

Set out a performance specification (minimum expected standards) for each for the following groups of people:

● wealthy western visitor
● local inhabitant
● someone looking for a balanced life style.

State who you think would have the best life style in which situation and outline your reasons why.

CIVILIZATION

When people's preoccupation with hunting turned to agriculture, it led to the growth of early civilizations and later to the ancient Greeks and Romans. This agricultural revolution, which began as long ago as 5000 BC, resulted in dramatic and fundamental changes to the structure and organization of society. This was reflected in the types of buildings constructed, which in turn reflected the nature of available materials and technology.

Relatively little is known about people living in prehistoric times. Fire, pigments and basic artefacts were some of the limited tools available. Expression (if it can be called that) in prehistoric cave paintings is especially remarkable given these severe limitations. Much more is known about ancient civilizations. Archaeology, writing, carving, art and sculpture reveal information about their nature and organization. Availability of materials and technology and their utilization are critical to any society. Early cities would almost certainly have been built using a combination of local materials – for example, stone, mud, early brick and timber etc. The closest we get to this today is adobe buildings in Mexico.

WORKPIECE 1.2

MATERIALS AND THEIR INFLUENCE ON DESIGN

The availability of materials is a key consideration for any modern development. Traditionally the use of available materials has been a determinant of building style and appearance. Consequently villages and towns in different localities and countries have different characteristics.

List three places which you know to have different characters in terms of their buildings.

List what these differences are.

Identify as many reasons as you can in relation to the availability of materials which have generated these characteristics.

Undertake the exercise above but use regions of three different countries.

As knowledge expanded about the construction and structure of buildings, agriculture, writing, art and so on, society changed. Religion and politics grew in influence. Economies evolved and developed. There are interesting conflicts and tensions between the emergence of religious beliefs and the way in which buildings, for example houses, evolved. Today architects and planners dream of and design (and occasionally build) ideal buildings and places – visionary forms for the ideal society. Has this always been the case? Which came first: the theory or the practice?

In his book *The Ancient City*,, Fustel de Coulanges discusses religious beliefs that generated social and political order. He describes the

VISION AND BUILDING

Identify a modern development which you believe has been generated as a result of an individual's vision of society.

Explain why you think this is the case.

List three historic buildings which have been created or heavily influenced by:

- a single individual;
- a group of people sharing common values and beliefs;
- a government institution.

Set out your reasons for identifying each. Discuss their importance/contribution to society as a whole.

organization of the courtyard house and how it evolved from these beliefs. He traces how inheritance derived from hereditary worship as follows (greatly simplified and shortened):

> According to the Greeks the sacred fire taught men to build houses. It is the man's duty to maintain fire. When the man dies the inheritance passes on to the next man in line to keep the hearth burning. The hearth is a central feature of the house around which the courtyard and dwelling are arranged with the Gods placed either side of the hearth thus giving symmetry to the plan.[1]

An alternative and equally abbreviated argument might run:

> Technology has advanced. Limited building spans have become possible for simple domestic dwellings. The easiest and most economical way to build a house is to construct a wall along the four sides of a square and pitch a simple roof off the wall, thereby creating a simple enclosure around a courtyard.

Which comes first: the ideas, political and religious beliefs, social organization and needs, or the technology to answer the question and solve the problems?

In today's society we are faced with what is, to many, an alarming pace of change. Innovation is a priority in many fields. In order to understand some of the processes leading to innovation and change, they can be categorized under three headings: opportunity, capacity and pressure.[2] These processes are important and are discussed elsewhere. They highlight our understanding as to whether ideas or practice come first in the cycle of creativity.

The dichotomy between theory and practice, between ideas and necessity, is a fundamental challenge to the way we work. Security, comfort, access, availability of materials, knowledge of building and invention in the form of necessity are as important as social order, politics and religious beliefs when creating appropriate places in which to live, work and feel comfortable.

LUNAR MODULE AND GOTHIC CATHEDRAL – A COMPARISON

Do we face the same problems today as we have always done? What are the major generators behind such diverse structures as Gothic cathedrals and lunar spacecraft? Are there parallels and common problems between the two? What are their similarities and differences?

In a famous speech to Congress in May 1961 President Kennedy urged the American people to aim for the moon as a matter of priority. He made it a national goal for the USA to land a man on the moon before the end of the decade. At 4.18 p.m. on 20 July 1969 the first manned

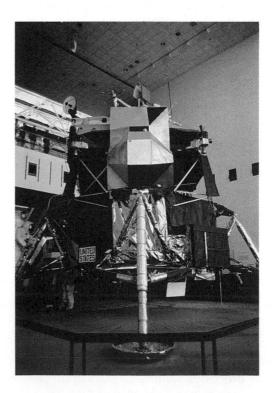

Figure 1.3   Lunar module. (Tom Muir.)

lunar landing took place. In November 1969 the second landing occurred so that by the end of the decade not one but two moon landings had been accomplished.[3] This extraordinary feat of mobilizing people's will, creating the technology and fulfilling a vision is perhaps one of the greatest technological achievements of any nation in peacetime this century. But how different was President Kennedy's declaration to that of a mediaeval bishop commissioning a Gothic cathedral that would dominate the local economy, community, business and industry for perhaps one hundred years?

This may seem an absurd comparison. But in order to understand the extraordinary forces that influence our daily lives and the nature of the development and construction industry, we need to make such comparisons. Surprisingly there are many similarities. Naturally there are also obvious differences.

WORKPIECE 1.4

GOTHIC CATHEDRAL AND LUNAR MODULE

The table below sets out 12 points by which we can compare these two extremes. The first nine are filled in. Do you agree with these points? The last three are left blank. What else does a Gothic cathedral have in common with the lunar module?

A comparison

Gothic cathedral	Spacecraft (lunar module)
1. Stretched known technology to the limit.	Stretched known technology to the limit.
2. Involved and impacted on the whole of the community.	Involved and impacted on society as a whole.
3. Part of power politics	Part of power politics
4. Involved thousands of people/craftsmen.	Involved tens of thousands of people/businesses.
5. Decreed by religious figure	Decreed by politicians (race to moon – 10 years, Kennedy)
6. Aspired to the 'heavens'	Man's first journey away from the earth
7. Structure must support extraordinary loads.	Structure must cope with huge forces
8. Load spread by foundations	Load spread by foundations
9. Structure supports skin	Structure supports skin.
10.	
11.	
12.	

Some of the comparisons are very obvious; for example, all buildings have foundations. Others however raise wider social and economic questions. The impact of a Gothic cathedral on its local community would have been enormous. Thousands of artisans and labourers would have been involved bringing employment to hundreds of associated

Figure 1.4   Gothic cathedral, Milan. (Tom Muir.)

trades and people. The sheer scale of the cathedral would have dwarfed all the surrounding buildings as it 'rose' towards the heavens. Stylistically the building would have made an impact on the character of neighbouring buildings. But most of all the Gothic cathedrals were extraordinary feats of technology, combining innovative approaches to materials with new structural concepts. Their approach to glazing involved enormous stained glass windows which were effectively one of the earliest forms of glass curtain walling.[4]

In many ways the lunar programme made an impact in a similar manner. The logistical demands of coordinating thousands of scientists and engineers and hundreds of different businesses in a common endeavour, which had never been tried before, affected the lives of millions of people. The lunar programme had clear political – as opposed to religious – goals and was very much a part of global power politics. The scale of the project was immense. The structure and skin of the orbiter and module had to withstand exceptional pressures and forces. Unimaginable conditions had to be allowed for in a web of back-up systems. And at the simplest level the lunar module had foundations (in its case highly sensitive computer assisted pads) – just like any building.

These two structures exemplify how design, technology and the development process are interwoven with each other. They also indicate the wealth of social, political and religious ideas that generate buildings and designs and how these ideas can influence economic growth and development.

Other comparisons could equally be made, for example between a bathyscope or submarine and a hospital, or between a mediaeval castle and a modern university.

BROAD COMPARISONS

Identify the two most different buildings you can think of.

List their similarities.

List their differences.

Discuss and analyse what generates these similarities and differences.

What other comparisons can be made? Identify the buildings or structures from two different cultures or parts of the world and compare their similarities and differences. How have religious beliefs and social need impacted on both? What was the economic impact? How does the design or visual appearance reflect cultural issues?

PROFESSIONAL VALUES

The development process can start in many ways. It can result from a designer persuading others that his or her idea is something that should be built. But far more often buildings and developments will come about as a result of a more complex set of reasons. A problem with some professionals today is that each likes to think their contribution is not only at the heart of the industry but also the most important in society. Such attitudes are misplaced. The essential ingredients for anyone wishing to play a major role in the environment or in society are team working and leadership. Leadership does not come about as a result of professional labels but leadership qualities can be encouraged through education and training. Working in a team is often underplayed in education yet it is an essential part of working life. These issues are important. They are dealt with largely elsewhere in this series (primarily in Book 3, *Management and Business Skills in the Built Environment*). They impinge directly on design, technology and the development process and can have all sorts of effects. Who would have predicted that the space race – a development process promoted for political reasons – would have resulted in the non-stick frying pan? What a wonderful example of how a very specific and detailed design problem (how to stop food sticking to the bottom of frying pans) was solved.

Both the Gothic cathedral and the race to the moon demanded huge investments of resources. The sheer costs were staggering. Both required dramatic commitments from leaders as well as society as a whole. What sort of value for money did they give?

11

Understanding finance and evaluating costs pose fundamental questions about the nature, use and purposes of technology and their value to society. Cost is a part of the equation. A cheap building may appeal to a client in the short term but cost much more in the long term. It may be less safe, deteriorate more quickly – hence require greater maintenance, or not totally fulfil all its requirements.

When prehistoric people embellished their caves with paintings – for whatever reason – it cost more in terms of time and materials than leaving the walls bare.[5] Much mediaeval building was only tested when under construction. Towers fell down, vaults collapsed, apses caved in. The mediaeval master builders had limited means of estimating the risks and calculating the loads. Yet the technological achievements of these sophisticated buildings were outstanding. The costs were high but how they have lasted and what delight they give today. Was this extraordinarily good value for money?

In contrast, preparations for the lunar landing were calculated and devised using the most sophisticated equipment and tests. It cost billions of dollars. There has always been a question as to whether or not this presented good value. It may have done so for the politicians but what about the poor in society, the starving nations – what good did it do them? However, the space programme never set out to address issues of poverty or distribution of wealth, although there were economic spin-offs. The programme was largely about power, influence and the utilization of modern technology. How many buildings and places are generated for the same reasons? (The word 'places' in this context means several buildings together with their intervening spaces). In its own way, did landing a man on the moon also result in good value for money?

Judgements about value and costs are critical. They affect our everyday lives. Can we as a society afford to build only the cheapest? Are we bankrupt of artistic and cultural values? How do we measure the long-term costs of buildings against short-term priorities, or for example the cost or value of decoration and artistic expression against financial return.

Islamic nations are among those who still place a substantial emphasis on investment in buildings as a demonstration of their faith. You have only to look around cities in the UK to see that some of the new landmarks are mosques.

THE INTELLECTUAL CHALLENGE

One of the great intellectual challenges we face today in the West is how to design in a largely secular society. Many of the great historical traditions in building have been generated by deep religious and philosophical

VALUES

Are we as a society bankrupt of artistic and cultural values? How do we measure the long-term costs of buildings against short-term priorities? What value can be placed on decoration and artistic expression against financial return?

These questions are as important as any in the process that connects design, technology and development.
Discuss.

beliefs. This applies as much to landscape architecture as it does to building design and civil engineering projects. But these beliefs do not exist today. In some parts of the world there are strong religious attitudes which underpin the whole direction and fabric of society. However, even in strongly religious societies there is often a gap between traditional attitudes to buildings and their design.

Many who have travelled to the Middle or Far East, or other areas where historically there have been very strong local building traditions, are dismayed to see that these roots have been swept aside in an avalanche of mediocre modern buildings. Why should this be so? What have we done to deserve such banality? Is it to do with the fragmentation of society and the polarization of professionals from the context in which they work?

All over the world there are excellent examples of modern buildings celebrating cultural diversity and the wide range of roots in design.

However, they are the exception rather than the rule. There are plenty of multi-cultural cities which have wonderful opportunities to celebrate their rich diversity and ethnic mix. But few have been able to create satisfactory environments that respond to their wealth of cultural influences and origins.

Wherever we are we need a framework to assess, analyse and solve problems. We need to utilize design and technology to the full. Any framework must embrace:

- social, political and economic questions;
- cultural questions;
- spiritual and religious questions.

It must also take account of physical comfort needs including keeping warm, dry and clean, and reflect the means by which civilizations create buildings, towns and cities that:

● express contemporary values;
● enhance spiritual as well as physical conditions;
● are uplifting; and
● are places and spaces in which people can relax and enjoy themselves.

The purpose of any critical framework is to assist in our understanding of the world around us and therefore to enhance the utilization of the world's resources through the application of design and technology. To achieve our framework we need to ask questions of ourselves and of each other. Whatever our role – as architect, builder, engineer, surveyor, planner, landscape architect, estate manager or other – we need to be not only knowledgeable about certain facts about the built environment but also critically aware. We need to understand ideas that shape buildings and places; technical ideas, about keeping warm and dry, about what

WORKPIECE 1.7

TOWARDS A FRAMEWORK

Twenty questions to assist in developing a critical framework for understanding the relationships between design and technology and their place in society.

About technology:

● How do we keep out the cold?
● How do we keep out the rain?
● How do we make a building stand up?
● How do we stop damp from the earth rising up through the building?
● How do we create warmth?
● How do we maintain warmth?
● How do we let in light?
● How do we respond to different climatic conditions?

About design:

● How do we make buildings look attractive?
● Why do we make buildings look attractive?
● Why do buildings from different periods look different?
● What affects the look of a building?

● What generates the design of a building?

About the development process:

● Why are some buildings more valuable than others?
● How does society control the development of buildings, towns and places?
● How do we place value on buildings?
● What cultural value do buildings and places have?
● What influence does the construction industry have on the national economy?
● What is the cost of a building to society?
● What is the value of a building to society?

From whatever angle you come to them, all these questions are inextricably bound up with issues of design, technology and the development process.

Which questions are the most important? List them in order of priority, briefly indicating in two or three short sentences your reasons for the placing of each priority. Are there other more important questions?

makes a building perform well physically. We must be aware of cultural, social, economic and political ideas and about how to organize buildings together to create places that are uplifting, that people can afford and will enjoy using. Consideration also needs to be given to the physical context of buildings, their geographical location and their setting in the landscape or in towns and in cities amongst other buildings. These are some of the issues we shall be exploring in this book.

The elements of building and development concern physical and practical skills. They consist of materials such as bricks, joists, roofing materials and components like walls, floors and ceilings. However, the utilization of these elements (how they are put together to satisfy the needs of clients, funders and users) is one of the greatest intellectual challenges that there is. The way in which this is undertaken has an effect on the lives of everyone, not just built environment professionals.

The development process may start with legislation, strategic planning or economic development and end with what may seem mundane details like the height of the ceiling or the colour of walls but it always reflects the utilization and application of design and technology. This applies as much to the setting of the building in the landscape, as it does to its construction.

Details such as eaves, floors, walls, ceilings, junctions and foundations do not only solve technical problems. They are also manifestations of social, political and cultural ideals and goals. Different periods have used different styles. The details of a building always perform particular tasks. They also reflect the period when they were created.

We have already compared a Gothic cathedral and the lunar module in terms of their structure and construction, but what about their setting? The lunar capsule was of course designed for an exceptionally barren environment; nevertheless, the use of design and technology in space research has influenced some modern architects in the way they think about buildings in their location. The geographical location of many of the great cathedrals was a key consideration in their design and construction. Durham Cathedral, with its stunning location on a hilly promontory protected on three sides by the River Wear, was an ideal location for the resting place of St Cuthbert's bones. York and Canterbury were historically both key cities during the period in which they established their religious significance.

There are many examples where a building's setting – the landscape – has become much more important than the building itself. The garden of Claude Monet (the leading impressionist painter) is a wonderful place in its own right, closely following traditional formal patterns of French gardening. Of course many people visit the garden because it was immortalized in Monet's paintings and the house because it was where he lived. Nevertheless the garden – as an expression of French culture and the setting for a house that is not particularly distinguished as a building – is an important piece of landscape in its own right. This is true of many famous gardens like Hidcote in England, Plas-yn-Rhiw on the Lleyn Peninsula in Wales and of course the Japanese gardens where landscape and buildings are integrated into an essential whole.

In the following chapters we shall be looking at many different aspects of design, technology and the development process including the way buildings have evolved through history and their relationship to the land. We shall be comparing elements that make up buildings and looking at the way different societies have handled similar problems. We shall not be doing this from the perspective of any single profession or viewpoint. On the contrary, we shall be exploring and comparing different ideas and approaches to find common goals between all the built environment professions and a means of ensuring that, whatever our role, we are united by these goals that transcend individual professional labels.

SUMMARY

Issues about the relationships between design, technology and the development processes are fundamental to any society. Even in earliest times people needed to express their spiritual and creative aspirations in their buildings. The availability and use of materials has influenced design, as indeed has society, through legislation, regulations and politics. Comparisons have been made to illustrate that there are common problems and issues even in extremely different buildings.

In order to understand design, technology and the development process we need to be able to analyse and assess buildings and their context. Everyone involved in the built environment should have a critical framework for analysing problems and solving them. The workpieces aim to encourage you to analyse these issues for yourself and in the last workpiece to start to establish your own critical framework.

Through the chapter we have:

- identified and distinguished between generators of buildings;
- identified environmental conditions that buildings must modify;
- explored cultural, social, political and other constraints which impact on buildings;
- introduced concepts and information which underpin this book.

The exercises have provided an opportunity to develop skills and attitudes which will assist in making judgements and decisions about the built environment.

- In the creation of buildings and places design, technology and the development process are all clearly interrelated.
- Intervention is about problem solving.
- Society needs buildings which are artistically rewarding and reflect cultural values as well as buildings that are economically viable and technologically sound.
- All buildings have to solve a significant number of common problems.
- Buildings reflect power.
- Individuals as well as groups can influence the built environment.
- All ages have generated important innovative works.
- Design and the use of technology are only a part of a wider process.
- Buildings in their details reflect the nature of the societies which created them.

1. Fustel de Coulanges, N.D. (1956), *Ancient City*, Doubleday, New York.
2. Carter, C.E. and Williams, B.R. (1957) *Industry and Technical Progress*, Oxford University Press.
3. Kerrod, R. (1989) *The Illustrated History of Man in Space*, Prion.
4. McCauley, D. (1970) *Cathedral, The story of its construction*, Collins & Co. Ltd.
5. Grand, P.M. (1967) *Prehistoric Art, Paleolithic Painting and Sculpture*, Studio Vista.

Architecture Exposed (1989) *All Helman Breaks Loose*, Arcus Ltd.
Biesty, S. (1993) *Incredible Cross-sections*, Dorling Kindersley.
Mann, A.T. (1993) *Sacred Architecture*, Element.
Nuttgens, P. (1983) *The Story of Architecture*, Phaidon.

2

THE SOCIAL CHALLENGE

ALAN MIDDLETON

THEME

The development process can be triggered in many ways –
through the ideas of an individual person, through collective
views of society, the planning process or a known industrial
or commercial need. Clients and users are central to this
process. Wherever it starts (or finishes) the process involves
intervention with the environment. So, what are the generators? Are they economic, social, political, the need to modify climate or what? Here contrasting interventions are used
to explore some of the fundamental generators of the
design and the development process. These are set in a
context of global issues and the way in which governments
can encourage sound building policies.

OBJECTIVES

After reading this chapter, you should have an understanding of
the variety of influences which generate and sustain the development process. You should be able to:

- understand the basic principles of the development process;

- identify the processes by which buildings and places are
  generated;

- identify problems in a global context;

- understand how governments can influence building development.

This chapter is about the complex interrelationships of the many and diverse forces which lie behind the development process. The creation of buildings or spaces is often celebrated as the imaginative work of creative individuals who transform artistic and scientific ideas into our physical environment. Wren's St Paul's Cathedral, Rogers' Pompidou Centre and Williams-Ellis's Portmeirion are examples of buildings and spaces which are instantly connected with their designers in the minds of large sections of the public. On the other hand, some landmark buildings achieve notoriety as 'carbuncles' on our townscape. In these cases, designers are also the focus of attention and attract the criticism of commentators. Most of our built environment is, however, unremarkable and it is in the study of what we take for granted that the complexity of the development process is laid bare.

Of what, then, is the built environment a product? Is it the product of the designer, engineer or professional team? What are the social and economic forces, political and cultural traditions that create the environment we know? This chapter sets out the broad social challenges that are sometimes forgotten about in the development process and relates them to specific building types. It identifies the net of contextual complexity in which as professionals we operate and through which occasionally great designers, remarkable buildings and monumental failures manage to rise above or slip through.

These fundamental challenges are enlarged upon in the following chapter which discusses in greater detail the impact of technology on society, its relationships with social change and its influence on building design. Then in Part Two we look at the development process and in Part Three the design and construction of buildings.

We shall first look at some of the social and economic forces which condition the creation of the built environment in the modern world, before going on to consider the roles that technological development, government and the professions have to play.

One of the greatest influences on the development of our physical environment is the simple movement of people. Rural to urban migration, usually in search of work, is possibly the greatest generator of demand for new urban places in the developing world today, just as it was in nineteenth century Britain at the time of the industrial revolution. As rural populations continue to grow and technological advances in agricultural production force more and more people off the land, the rural poor become the dispossessed of expanding urban centres, stimulating a demand for shelter which local resources cannot adequately meet. In

INTRODUCTION

SOCIAL FORCES

the first instance, this can result in the transmission of rural designs and materials to the poorer settlements of Third World cities, even though their inhabitants may aspire to the standards of the developed world and Third World elites.[1]

The impact of internal migration can also be exacerbated by international population movements, which are often the result of crises and conflict. The Irish famine of the 19th century and the expulsion of Jews from Central Europe in the 19th and 20th centuries created ethnic enclaves in the developing cities of Europe of the time. The slaughter of Muslims, Hindus and Sikhs which followed the partition of India in 1947 created a mass movement and a demand for housing, which was partially met through the generation of the first squatter settlements in South Asia, religious buildings and workplaces.[2] The economic migration of Italians, Poles and Irish to the United States, from the nineteenth century onwards, created ethnic enclaves with physical characteristics which reflected their cultures and religions and which persist to the present day. The black population of the Chota Valley in Ecuador, whose forefathers were transported to South America to work in the sugar plantations, live in houses which are similar in design to those found in the part of West Africa from which they originated. The tribal conflicts in Rwanda in 1994 have created a cross-border movement, which will generate a new crisis of shelter in neighbouring countries that will have to be met mainly through the use of local resources.

Figure 2.1 Mass population movement: refugees from Rwanda on the road to Benaco camps. (Mission Aviation Fellowship UK.)

On the other hand, the movement of a relatively small number of colonialists has often had far greater impact on the urban and rural environment than mass movements of the poor and dispossessed. Bringing with them a concept of ownership which divides up communal agricultural land for semi-feudal and capitalist production methods, introducing new forms and techniques of production which have an impact on the natural environment and often displace people from the rural areas, the colonialists also bring their design concepts as expressed in urban and rural buildings and the layout of major cities. The Spanish-style hacienda of South America, the religious buildings of successive waves of Sikh and Moghul conquest in the Indian subcontinent, and the railway stations, government buildings and gridiron street patterns of the British cantonment which followed in imperial India and other cities in the developing world are all examples of the influence of powerful invaders on local built form.[2]

Normally, however, the resultant built environment is a mixture of influences, which are often to be found in single buildings such as the railway station in Kuala Lumpur or the law courts in Lahore. This influence is not, of course, totally one way, as the introduction of the Malaysian bungalow into colonial culture and its subsequent dissemination to the UK and other colonial cultures testifies.

Figure 2.2 Kuala Lumpur railway station, showing mixture of influences but set amidst bland modern development. (Tony Collier.)

The type of shelter which is required depends on who migrates. It is mainly the young who migrate and if the migration is predominantly of young single people, the demand is likely to be for single rooms; whereas if the tendency is for young families to move to the urban areas, this will stimulate a demand for larger units. Over time, family size is likely to increase creating new demands for such buildings as larger houses, schools and health centres.

Figure 2.3 Simple dwellings in Lahore made from any available material. (Alan Middleton.)

MIGRATION

In developing countries today, the tendency is for migrants to move to central areas of cities so that they can be close to work opportunities. Initially, they will rent and share accommodation. Once they have found a niche in the urban labour market, settled down and started a family, they may move to their own house in more peripheral locations, often to squatter settlements which lack basic infrastructure and services.[3] In order to supplement their meagre incomes, the home may also become a workplace, creating a demand for a different type of space. As children grow older and family size increases further, the need to separate the sexes has a further impact on housing needs.

However, migration is not merely confined to history in the

developed world. In post-war Britain, migration has taken place both as an instrument of public policy and as a response to economic change. As city centre slums were cleared, peripheral estates and new towns were created by central and local government.[4] Populations moved away from the inner cities by planned action and as the economic fortunes of older cities declined it was mainly the young who moved elsewhere in search of employment. In these growing settlements, the demand for schools, transport and health centres also increased, even where average family size remained constant.

The quality of the constructed environment that resulted reflected the level of resources that were put into these new settlements. The contrast between the quality of life in the peripheral housing estates of a city such as Glasgow and that of the new towns like Cumbernauld or East Kilbride could not be more stark.[5] Both types of settlement were characteristic of the public sector building boom of the 1950s and 1960s.

The former were built as dormitory settlements of the cities, with a minimum of investment in shopping, leisure and health facilities and an almost complete absence of employment opportunities. The latter were originally conceived as free-standing towns which would require large-scale investment. In fact, the new towns did not become entirely free-standing, with residents travelling out of the area to work and others from outside travelling in for the same purpose, but the commitment to the concept was sufficient to ensure a level of investment and subsequent quality of life which was denied to the residents of the peripheral estates.

As the slums of cities like Glasgow were cleared, allocation policies served to exacerbate the differences between the two types of settlement. Those who could find employment in the modern industries of the new towns were given preferential treatment in the allocation of housing. This attracted the skilled working class or office workers and left a disproportionate number of those who were unskilled and in insecure employment to the 'deserts with windows' on the urban peripheral estates.

Over time, as the British economy has gone through cyclical recessionary periods in a downward spiral of decline, the gap between the unemployment rates and household incomes of these two types of settlement have increased. The result is visible in the standard of the shopping and other facilities which exist.

In the new towns, as in all new settlements, the demand for certain types of building varies over time. For the young families who moved to these settlements in the first waves of migration, the availability of primary schools for their children was of considerable importance. As the children grew, their educational needs were met by accessible secondary schools and usually a local college, although those who went on to higher education would travel to the cities. As the population matures, the demand for primary education declines and schools are closed or put to other uses. If the population continues to grow in numbers and the town expands in space, the schools are usually in the wrong place. Health and community care for the elderly becomes an issue, as does youth training, creating a demand for a new type of building which can sometimes be met by the conversion of redundant schools. However, school closure by a local authority inevitably meets with community resistance.

COMMUNITY INVOLVEMENT

The level of community involvement in the development process varies considerably over time, from one area to another, from city to city and from country to country.[6] Mature residents are more likely to be committed to the communities in which they live than the young and they are more likely to participate in groups which can influence the future development of the built environment. Women are more likely to participate than men, in struggles over housing in particular. Community groups, however, are often transitory, particularly if organized around single issues which are resolved. Built environment professionals such as planners have a statutory duty, and usually a professional and personal commitment, to promote public participation but the bureaucratic structures within which they operate make it difficult for them to fulfil that commitment. For the bureaucrat, community organizations can be a thorn in the flesh. For the planner or architect, their demands can be aesthetically unpleasing or may sit uneasily with their professional training. The professional's technical skills are conditioned by cultural context, education and training, pressures of work, the demands of local politicians, peer group assessment, the influence of developers and wealthy elites, their own family and community needs and, not least, the distribution of power in society, all of which may influence their capacity to respond to the needs of local communities which are not their own.

ECONOMIC FORCES

The changes which have been taking place in the national and international economies also have a considerable effect on the built environment in the UK.[7] The changing structure of production, as investment

POST-WAR DEVELOPMENTS

In post-war Britain inner city slums were cleared and replaced by new housing estates and new towns. For a conurbation of your choice, identify:

● a post-war housing estate;
● a nearby new town.

What are the differences in:

● housing types and standards;
● shopping facilities;
● educational provision;
● accessibility to medical care;
● the green environment?

Can you identify the processes of growth which have contributed to these differences?

and employment shift from traditional large-scale manufacturing industries to small-scale activities in the service sector, implies a change in building types.

As steel mills and engineering works become redundant, they are pulled down to make way for green space, new shopping malls and high technology business parks. However, the changing structure of the economy also implies a reorientation of investment and employment in space. Increasingly the new buildings, often small in size and sometimes built to high specifications, are located outside the major cities in small towns and in the rural areas. Over the last 30 years there has also been a drift to the south east, away from the north.

As investment and jobs in older cities have declined, so have populations. The cities of Glasgow, Liverpool and Newcastle have been losing population over a considerable period. This has consequences for housing demand and for the future of shopping centres. Stigmatized parts of relatively new housing estates become surplus to requirements and fall into dereliction and unpopular high rise flats become difficult to let. As populations decline and as incomes fall, local shopping becomes unsustainable and recently constructed shopping parades become vacant and vandalized.

In contrast, since the new industries generally do not create the health and pollution hazards of those they replace and are therefore more acceptable in traditionally clean environments, their emergence in non-industrial Britain has further implications for the built environment. Additional employment is created in relatively employment-rich areas, raising the price of labour, creating work for women whose partners are also in work and, therefore, raising household incomes. This further stimulates demand for services, including shopping, thereby attracting more investment in buildings, more people into the area, and so on. With an increasing demand for housing, factory space and offices, the Green Belt can come under threat. Space has to be found for new housing and business parks and the most attractive and financially viable locations are green-field sites.

The countryside and the natural environment can also come under threat from mineral extraction activities, creating open-cast sites, pipelines which snake across the country, oil refineries and other installations of related chemical industries. Normally these industries in the developed world are required to return the land they disrupt to its original state. However, new activities in, for example, the oil industry are often unregulated in developing countries and can have a considerable direct impact on the built environment in other ways in the developed world.

DEVELOPING COUNTRIES

In the developing countries, environmental controls are less stringent than in Europe and North America and there are several examples of indigenous peoples taking the oil companies to international courts in search of damages. Third World governments are often reluctant to apply strict controls that would present a barrier to investment from multinational corporations, or indeed lead them to disinvest, and environmental pollution often results. However, a recent court judgement in the United States, in which the judge was guided by the declaration of the Rio Earth Summit of 1993, has meant that an indigenous group from the Ecuadorian Amazon region is able to claim damages in US courts, despite opposition from their own government. The importance of this judgement is that in future US companies which invest overseas will have to apply the same standards of construction and maintenance for oil installations and other potentially polluting factories as they would at home.

The impact of the extraction of mineral wealth goes beyond the extraction, transport and conversion of the product itself. As local jobs are generated, new settlements spring up, whether these be in the Grampian Region of Scotland or in Amazonia. New businesses spring up, serving the needs of the main extractive industry and/or the growing population. Transport infrastructure is created where it is needed to serve the industry, leading in the case of Amazonia to further immigration, population expansion, colonization of virgin rain forest, support industries, and so on. Mass rural-to-rural migration can take place with new buildings created from the materials of the rain forest and new sources of pollution seeping into the water tables and the rivers. The new settlements and infrastructure open up the potential for the further extraction of timber for the construction industry in the region and elsewhere. The uncontrolled encroachment of the artificial environment thereby threatens not only the local natural environment but also, through the effects of the destruction of the rain forests, the well-being of us all. The raising of the world's consciousness about these issues may yet have an impact on developments such as those above.

The economic impact of other types of international investor can also have an impact on local construction and development processes. Since the early 1980s, capital flows out of the UK have been considerable, as British companies and institutions have invested in North America and the Far East. At the same time, however, inward investment from foreign companies has had an impact on the built environment, through both the locations where they choose to invest and the way they manage the construction process.[8] Firstly, foreign manufacturers invariably look for green-field sites in attractive locations, thereby applying further pressure on the Green Belt. Secondly, they bring with them their own management styles and, to the extent that they become involved in the construction process, this has an impact on the way in which British construction professionals and workers relate to each other. For example, when Toyota decided to build an auto plant in Derbyshire, they hired a Japanese construction firm with whom they had a long-term relationship to manage the construction process. This firm brought with them a management style and a set of expectations which caused the British professionals who worked for them to reassess their traditional professional boundaries and expectations.

Not all countries have the same professional structure as the British construction industry and if foreign firms increasingly become involved in construction in this country, as is predicted, we should expect pressure to break down further traditional expectations about the role of the various professionals. To some extent this is beginning to happen in Britain without this external pressure.

One of the most important influences on the development process in any country is the pattern of land ownership.[9] The extent of its concentration in a few hands or its distribution amongst many has an influence on the ability and motivation of people to build and improve their housing, invest in industrial and commercial buildings in particular localities,

INWARD INVESTMENT

LAND OWNERSHIP

27

WORKPIECE 2.2

BUILDING TYPES

The changing structure of production in Britain has led to a demand for different types of building from that required by traditional manufacturing industries. Selecting an industrial area of the country, can you identify three different new uses to which redundant factories have been put?

What were the reasons for developers choosing these specific uses?

What types of new building have been constructed as a result?

Who was employed in the old factories (sex, skills, age, social class, etc.)?

Who is employed in the new units?

Have any of the new developments had an impact on the use of other buildings (such as traditional shopping centres)?

obtain finance for investment in buildings, and so on. Concentration of land ownership in rural areas of Latin America stimulates rural exodus to the cities as landowners invest in labour-saving machinery. A proliferation of small farms allows the absorption of family labour in a process which leads to the retention and impoverishment of rural households in dilapidated structures.

Ownership of land titles in urban areas in the Third World provides security and leads squatters to invest in the improvement of their dwellings. In fact, families who are secure in the knowledge that they will not be turned off the land, whether or not they are the legal owners, are much more likely to improve their houses and struggle for infrastructure upgrading than those who feel themselves to be under threat. They will also apply pressure on authorities for the construction of schools, health centres and other communal buildings.

Land banking, whereby the public sector or private firms hold on to land for speculative or future development purposes, can also influence the rate of development. Holding land from the market slows down the process, pushes up prices and increases the profits of companies if they pick the right time to sell or develop. Local authorities which hold land and refuse to sell for ideological reasons, as was the case with many Labour authorities in post-war Britain, can push up the price of private housing because of scarcity and can cause firms who might otherwise invest in a locality to invest elsewhere. Many large companies will only invest where they can become the owners of the land and buildings and the refusal of councils to release land to them has caused disinvestment and removal to other locations.

LAND OWNERSHIP

The ownership of land is a measure of wealth which can have a liberating effect on its owner or a constraining effect on tenants. The landlord–tenant relationship also implies responsibilities to each other. Make a list of what you think are:

● the reponsibilities of landowners to tenants in rural areas;
● the reponsibilities of landowners to leaseholders in urban areas.

Try to identify:

● the extent of leasehold and freehold properties in an English and Scottish city of your choice;
● how you would discover the major landowners in each city;
● what the relationship is of land values to residential property values in different areas of any city.

FINANCE

The nature of the finance system can also stimulate or hold back the property market. In the UK, banks are among the largest property owners and investment in land and buildings is a key activity of other actors in the financial sector, such as insurance companies and pension funds. Overseas banks were major investors in the remodelling of the City of London in the 1980s and a range of financial institutions became involved in the regeneration of docklands. Large-scale developments require the organization of consortia by the developers and this is sometimes done with the assistance and underwriting of local and central government agencies.

Grants and low interest loans are also available from central goverments and the European Union. In 1994, prior to the introduction of the Single Regeneration Budget which combined the resources from 20 different government programmes, there was a multitude of different sources of subsidy and support available for property development in British cities.

These funds, channelled through five ministries via, for example, urban development corporations, housing action trusts, inner city task forces, city action teams, city challenge boards, training and enterprise councils, regional enterprise grants, and so on, were supported by European finance such as European Regional Development Funds (ERDF), European Social Funds (ESF), European Coal and Steel Funds (ECSF) and further supplemented by local authority subsidies and investments which provide incentives to property developers to invest in different areas.

The existence of a housing finance system is of course crucial for the development of the housing market, but the nature of this may vary from country to country in the developed world and it may be non-existent in developing countries.

Finance systems may fund the construction and/or purchase of housing. In Britain these two functions have traditionally been separate, with private banks providing the main funds for construction and building societies financing the purchase of housing by potential owners. In countries where all the banks are nationalized, government-owned institutions may fund both; in others, the private sector may fund construction for sale on a speculative basis while the state may provide limited funds for the purchaser. Expectations about the contribution of individual savings to the total cost of a house can also vary widely from country to country. In Germany, for example, where home ownership is much lower than in Britain, it is expected that the purchaser will provide a much higher deposit than in Britain.

In developing countries, where the formal financial system is much less developed, informal systems often predominate. Informal financial systems exist in most countries, the most common being credit unions or rotating credit associations.[10] In the UK little use is made of these institutions for financing property development, but in the United States the savings from credit unions are more likely to be used for housing purposes. In developing countries these sources, along with savings, can be the main source of housing finance. In Nigeria, for example, they are used for buying houses not only by potential owner–occupiers but also by landlords of tenement rooming houses and flats.

WORKPIECE 2.4

SOURCES OF FINANCE

Identify a major property development in a British city of your choice and make a list of the sources of finance which would have been available for the project.

TECHNOLOGY

The development process is also conditioned by technological advances, both within the construction industry and in other areas of the economy. 'Traditional' building technology varies from country to country, reflecting the types of material that are available for construction, the climatic conditions of a particular area, the local culture, the level of economic development, and so on. Compare the pitched-roof Glasgow tenements with the flat-roofed adobe Mexican villa, the brick-built back-to-backs of Manchester and Birmingham, the bamboo houses built over the water of Brunei and swamps of Ecuadorian coastal cities. Each reflects a particular combination of skills, materials and needs that respond to local realities and they involve different production processes. Technological advances in materials are disseminated throughout the world and can be used by the élite in the construction of housing and by multinational firms in their offices and factories around the world.

Some technologies, however, do not travel well. The system-built flats which dominated British housing in the 1960s and 1970s are culturally unacceptable in many Muslim countries since their communal areas do not afford women the privacy they require around their homes, and they are unsuitable for hot climates without expensive air-conditioning.[11] With some adaptation, the same technologies can be suitable for office accommodation, but they have been rapidly overtaken by the steel and glass structures which now dominate flourishing urban city centres.

The structures of the 1960s are also no longer suitable for new office technologies. Floor-to-ceiling heights are no longer adequate as computerization and new communications systems require space to carry channels for information networks.[12] That is, communications technology demands new design standards and the new technology of the service sector of the 1990s requires innovative office design. Similarly, technological advances in manufacturing require different types of space from that which was needed under the old Fordist production systems, which were staff intensive, and controlled atmospheres for computerized systems have replaced the muck and grime of the foundry.

Advances in transport technology have reintroduced light rail transit systems in many urban centres and improvements in long-distance rail transport have made the Channel tunnel, and its passenger and freight terminals, a possibility. Just as the technological advances associated with containerization and port transport in the 1960s had a lasting detrimental impact on the fortunes of the docklands of Liverpool, London and Glasgow, while at the same time enhancing the fortunes of ports such as Southampton, the new rail technologies may redistribute the transport infrastructure and buildings in the last decade of the twentieth century. The impact of containerization on the built environment in the old centres of maritime transport was dramatic. The subsequent decline, however, also created opportunities for new uses for these areas.

WORKPIECE 2.5

DESIGN AND CONSTRUCTION

What is the range of factors which influence the design and construction of a school?

THE ROLE OF GOVERNMENT

We have seen above that government pursuit of a New Towns policy and the construction of peripheral estates in the 1950s and 1960s was to have a dramatic effect on the creation of new environments for ordinary people. In the 1960s and 1970s, central government provided financial support to local authorities and the construction industry in order to encourage technological change in house construction, resulting in the development of a high-rise policy and the rapid growth of system-built housing. Through the planning system, government also controls the use of land and buildings. Through fiscal measures and the use of regional policy, government can influence capital investment flows, both internally and internationally, and these in turn can influence the demand for certain types of building from industry and commerce and, through the creation of employment, influence population movement which creates further demand for housing, infrastructure and the buildings needed to provide support services. Government-supported agencies such as urban development corporations, city challenge boards and training and enterprise councils have been active in the supply of property and infrastructure in urban areas. As the direct supplier of some of the above services, such as education and health, government has direct control over the supply and design of buildings in expanding and declining communities. Through the provision of improvement grants, the quality of buildings can be sustained and enhanced.

Historically, urban governments in Britain have favoured slum clearance and reconstruction over the rehabilitation of old buildings. From the mid nineteenth century through to the 1970s, the clearance of slums and the promise of new housing was a major feature of city council activity. With industrial decline and falling populations, the 1980s brought a new imperative. Employment became a major concern. With the shift in the structure of the economy which had taken place, as manufacturing declined in importance the service sector increased and was seen to be necessary for city survival. Making the city attractive to mobile businesses therefore became a major feature of local authority activity. Improving the appearance of the city centre, through the cleaning of old buildings and the building of new ones, has become an essential ingredient for the promotion of 'business tourism'.

Supported by a number of central government initiatives, every city in the UK is now locked in competition for inward investment, with the result that the appearances of city centres are being improved and transformed by local authorities. Just as the damaging decline of the docks also provided opportunities to improve the built environment, the general decline associated with falling populations, slum clearance and the disappearance of the manufacturing base has made a new type of reconstruction possible. New convention centres, concert halls, exhibition centres and indoor sports arenas are to be found in or are planned for almost all major cities. In Birmingham, Glasgow, Manchester and Sheffield this approach has become a major issue.[13]

There are limits to local government expenditures in these fields. Central government controls the amount of borrowing that local authorities are allowed and, although innovative financial mechanisms have been devised by councils, the financial demands of these projects are in conflict with the capital needs of basic services such as education and housing. Stark choices have to be made. Should an authority fund prestige projects if it means diverting funds from the repair and refurbishment of school buildings and housing? For the councillors, city officials and professionals associated with the projects, the answer is yes; for the users of schools and those living in sub-standard housing, the answer will probably be different.

WORKPIECE 2.6

BENEFITS OF DEVELOPMENT

Try to create a list of property development projects which are currently supported by central government initiatives in a city of your choice.

Identify who the users of these projects are likely to be when they are completed.

What are the expected benefits for local people?

Who will gain employment in them?

What type of work will it be?

PROFESSIONALS

But what of the role of the built environment professional in this context – the architects who bring together art and science in the design of buildings; the planners with their concern for the protection of amenity, settlement lay-out and the use of land and buildings; the quantity surveyor whose main concern is with the economics of construction and the management of costs; the structural engineers with their focus on structures, mechanics and safety; the building surveyors with their concern for the physical maintenance of buildings; and the civil engineers who design and deliver both huge industrial projects and the infrastructural requirements for urban living? Firstly, for the delivery of any project they must work as a team within any organization, despite their competing professional outlooks and contributions. Secondly, they can often be on opposing teams representing private interests, community interests or, as government officers, the wider public interest.

In the private sector they will respond to the needs of clients and represent their interests wherever relevant. In the public sector they will seek to represent the interests of the general public, often through exercising control over private sector interests if these are seen to be in conflict with the general good. As representatives of community interests they will often be in conflict with both private and public sector colleagues, championing consumers of the built environment against profit orientation and bureaucracy. Trained as professionals in the same university schools, their practice as professionals will be conditioned by their personal ethics, moral standpoints, position in their organization, economic and job security, and a host of other personal and workplace considerations. They are also consumers of the built environments they create.

WORKPIECE 2.7

PROFESSIONAL ROLES

What are the roles of built environment professionals in the projects identified in Workpiece 2.6?

The conficting demands on the built environment professionals, however, mean that the relationship with the client, public and society is not a simple one. If we return to the context of changing social and economic structures and consider the influences on the design of a small building, the theory we have discussed comes to life. Population movements to a new community or the changing age structure of a settlement can create a demand for a new health centre or a new school. The design of these buildings will be influenced by the availability of finance and the technology which is available for both construction and the professional work of the building user. But the professional user is not the only user of these buildings and the needs of the non-professional user (patient or schoolchild) must be taken into account. The building technology which can be used will be conditioned by the amount of finance which is available for construction. The technology which the professional needs to carry out his or her duties may be subject to another budget and can make demands on space and the design concept. In the case of the health centre, the needs of the user-professional's clients (the patients) can influence the technological need and therefore the design of the building.

Figure 2.4 Lee Bank Health Centre, UK, designed by Associated Architects to meet changing needs and demands. (Alastair Carew-Cox.)

Both the doctor and the patient are the users of the buildings. The architect's client may be the doctor or a private group practice, but it could be the public health service which will be represented by a manager, usually from a different profession and with a different perspective on the construction process. This further confuses the question as to who is the client in this case. The patron–client relationship between architect and doctor is mediated by the professional–client relationship between doctor and patient and by a representative of the 'common good', who is responsible for taxpayers' money.

The final design of the health centre in a given socio-economic context will therefore depend on a variety of factors. Historical custom and practice in the design of such buildings will also have a considerable influence, as will changing government policy with respect to funding the health service; the size of the group practice and any expected increase or decline in the future; anticipated changes in the legislation which will influence the demand for medical services within the health centre; the planning constraints and building controls imposed by the local authority; and the balance between the finance which is available, the technology which is required for the efficient conduct of the doctor's professional responsibility, and the needs of the patient. However, the architect's aesthetic orientation is not only conditioned by these factors which impinge on the need to design for efficiency and at the same time for comfort and style; it is also influenced by a range of possible relationships with the building professionals and company owners who are responsible for construction on site.

SUMMARY

In this chapter we have looked at the social, economic, cultural, technological and political forces that lie behind the generation of demand for buildings. Starting from the assumption that most of the built environment is unremarkable, we have noted the impact of the movement of people on the demand for buildings and the transmission of design. Mass movements in times of political crisis, migration for economic reasons, colonist expansion and the planning of new towns and peripheral housing estates have all had an impact on the type of shelter that is developed, as well as the generation of schools, health centres, shopping and other service facilities. Demand for buildings varies over time, as does the level of community involvement in the design and development process.

Changing economic circumstances create new demands for buildings, making others redundant. The decline of older industrial areas and investment in new service industries on the peripheries of cities and in other parts of the country change the urban and rural built environment, often threatening the natural environment in the process. Patterns of land ownership, security of tenure, the possibility of multiple ownership of land and land banking practices also have an impact on the design and development of the built environment.

The organization of the finance system is also important, particularly the housing finance system, and in developing countries informal sources of finance are crucial. Technology for construction varies in time and space, responding to local climate and cultural conditions, and its transferability is problematical.

The role of government is central, even in market economies, through the planning system, the promotion of different types of housing policy, economic policy and the direct provision of services such as education and health. Built environment professionals, in competition and cooperation, can represent competing interests in the development process. This interaction takes place in the context of their different professional training and a host of personal and organizational considerations.

The design and delivery of 'ordinary' buildings and the spaces between them is therefore a complex process. It is the product of many competing forces which are ultimately expressed in the relationship between the people who finance, design, construct, and use the built environment.

KEY CONCEPTS

- Most of our built environment is the product of not only designers but also a complexity of social and economic forces, political and cultural traditions, technological developments, negotiations between professionals, climatic imperatives, the availability of materials, and so on.
- One of the greatest influences on the development of the physical environment is the movement of people.
- The type of people who move has an impact on the demand for different types of building.
- The changing structure of the national and international economy influences decline and development in time and space, through the reorientation of investment and employment.
- This reinvestment can have a detrimental effect on the natural environment.
- Patterns of land ownership, land banking and security of tenure affect the pace and nature of development.
- The nature of the finance system, which can vary considerably, both within the developed world and between developed and less developed countries, can stimulate or hold back the property market.
- The development process is conditioned by technological advances, both within the construction industry and in other areas of the economy, but many technologies do not transfer easily into other cultures and climates.

- The influence of government remains central, even within the market economies.
- Built environment professionals, operating within the above contextual complexity, may bring their professional expertise to bear in the interest of the public sector, the private sector and/or the community, often expressing personal preferences and workplace pressures.

REFERENCES

1. Roberts, B. (1978) *Cities of Peasants*, Edward Arnold.
2. Qudeer, M.A. (1983) *Lahore: Urban Development in the Third World*, Vanguard Books.
3. Turner, J.F.C. (1976) *Housing by People; Towards Autonomy in Building Environments*, Marion Boyers.
4. Donnison, D. and Middleton, A. (1978) *Regenerating the Inner City*, Routledge and Kegan Paul.
5. Middleton, A. (1984) Cumbernauld: Concept, Compromise and Organizational Conflict. *Built Environment*, Vol. 9, No.3/4, 218–239.
6. Wilcox, D. (1994) *The Guide to Effective Participation*, Partnership Books.
7. Dickens, P. (1992) *Global Shift: The Internationalization of Economic Activity*, Paul Chapman.
8. Fothergill, S., Monk, S. and Perry, M. (1987) *Property and Industrial Development*, Hutchinson.
9. Healey, P. (1952) Urban Regeneration and the Development Industry, in Healey, P. *et al.* (eds) *Rebuilding the City: Property-led Urban Regeneration*, E & FN Spon.
10. Osondu, I.N. and Middleton, A. (1994) *Informal Housing Finance in Nigeria*, paper presented to ENHR conference on Housing in Developing Countries, Birmingham.
11. Middleton, A. and Hughes, G. (1990) *Planning and Low-cost Housing in Pakistan*, Research Paper No. 5, Faculty of the Built Environment, Birmingham Polytechnic (now University of Central England).
12. Middleton, A. *et al.* (1990) *The Proposed Redevelopment of the Bull Ring, Birmingham*, Built Environment Development Centre, Birmingham Polytechnic (now University of Central England).
13. Loftman, P. and Nevin, B. (1992) *Urban Regeneration and Social Equity: A Case Study of Birmingham*, Research Paper No. 8, Faculty of the Built Environment, University of Central Birmingham.

FURTHER READING

Fonstein, S.S., Gordon, I. and Harloe, M. (1992) *Divided City: New York and London in the Contemporary World*, Blackwell.

Logan, J.R. and Molotch, H.L. (1987) *Urban Futures: The Political Economy of Place*, University of California Press.

THE CHALLENGE OF TECHNOLOGY

DAVID BOYD

Technology and social change are interrelated. Technology poses fundamental challenges to society and in turn built environment professionals. This chapter seeks to develop the way we think about technology and our understanding of these challenges. It does so as a basis for promoting our general appreciation of the nature of society and the place of technology in it and also in order to establish our way of thinking about technology in relation to building design, which will be further explored in Part Three.

The extraordinary pace of technological change is a major concern. How are these changes influencing the built environment? What implications do they have for the design and development process? How will society – and government – promote them for the benefit of society as a whole? What is the relationship between these kinds of change, the needs of developing countries and new low cost techniques for building and construction?

It is interesting that we can talk about technology separately from our society and our natural world. It gives us the feeling that technology is something external waiting to be discovered, whereas technology is intimately linked with the historical developments of society in a political and economic way. We have all been brought up on media that look for 'gee whiz' stories and the success of technology has provided ample entertainment. On the other hand, worries have been punching through this rosy picture in the form of environmental damage, resource depletion, and human degradation. As professional people, it is our responsibility to use, develop and cope with technology. We must be able to forge a path through the rhetoric, the myths, the hyperbole, the self-interest and the economic imperative. This requires an understanding of the impact of technology which this chapter starts to provide.

OBJECTIVES

After reading this chapter you should be able to:

● understand technology in a broader historical, social, political and environmental context;

● use a technique of technological impact analysis;

● understand the impact of a number of technologies associated with the built environment;

● appreciate the concept of appropriate technology and how this is important for both the developing and the developed world.

INTRODUCTION

Although buildings use technology in their materials, construction and operation, they are seen as being somewhat primitive. It is the high technology that transforms power, speed, strength, size and innovation that arrests our imagination. It is the impact of this high technology in the form of computers and communications that has heralded what has been called the second industrial revolution. However, to understand the impact of technology, we must avoid being drawn into this almost surreal world where we are not sure what is real and what is imagined; where everything is possible and everything is wonderful.

Technology and science are something of a paradox. They provide us with security in food, health, energy, transport, a range of labour-saving artefacts and now information and communications technology. On the other hand, the development and use of technology has yielded problems of pollution, resource depletion, animal extinction, new diseases, weapons of mass destruction and inhuman social relations. The impact of technology is therefore ambiguous; some of it is good, some of it is bad. Further, some of it can be good and bad at the same time, if viewed from the perspectives of different people, or viewed in the short term and long term by the same people. Are the benefits of technology associated with buildings also ambiguous? We shall see that they are and that the apparent simplicity and benignity of building technology can hide major changes in the nature of buildings. Thus, the impact of technology is not only an issue about resources and the application of science but something that raises political and moral questions. The answers may be influenced by who you are, where you live or which part of the world you come from.

Technology is viewed generally as an artefact or tool for the performance of a function. However, technology is not the sum of these components; of the bricks and beams, glass and boilers, mastics and computers. It is a part of our life and very existence. It involves organizations, procedures, symbols, vocabulary, equations and, fundamentally, the way we think about the world. The pervasive influence of technology makes it difficult for us to determine and assess its impact without placing it in its historic, political and social context. But how do we assess the impact of technology? One method that we shall be looking at is technology assessment (TA), which originated from America.

Building and building technology have a long-term impact. This may not be detectable within a generation. In this chapter we shall look at the impact of some technologies and their influence on buildings. We will also look at the relationship of technology to the developing world. The rewards, and problems, of technology are more acute and less equitable in these countries; thus, we have a responsibility to understand the nature of the impact of technology transfer from the industrialized countries to those struggling for survival. In doing this analysis, the concept of an appropriate technology which respects the society and environment in which it is used will be considered. It will be concluded that such an understanding may be equally important in the developed world.

By placing technology in its historical context we can understand the roots of more recent technological changes and assess their future consequences. Table 3.1 shows a chronological list of technological and building events. The earliest technology included such artefacts as stone axes and shelters built from branches and turf. The Greeks, and particularly the Romans, had a well-developed technological infrastructure and ways of thinking. They had the ability to make concrete, to design, manage and construct large projects and to provide a level of comfort in their dwellings.

A SHORT HISTORY OF TECHNOLOGY

Table 3.1 Chronological list of technological and building developments

		1792	Gas lighting
		1829	Iron framed warehouse
		1834	Refrigeration compressor
		1839	Centrifugal pump
		1850	Mechanical fan ventilation
		1851	Crystal Palace Exhibition
		1852	Electric heating
		1854	Reinforced concrete
		1859	First building with lift
1876	Bell invents telephone	1880	Extract ventilation
			Filament lamp
		1882	Domestic fridge
1885	Benz first petrol car	1889	Eiffel Tower
		1890	Steel framed building
1901	Marconi Radio		
1903	First flight		
		1906	Concept of air-conditioning
1909	First plastic, Bakelite		
1914–	WW1, Tanks, Gas warfare		
1918		1919	Bauhaus Movement
			Use of air-conditioning in cinema
1920	Radio broadcasting		
		1927	First air-conditioned office
1936	Television broadcasting		
1939–	WW2, Radar, jet aircraft,		
1945	atomic bomb, first computer	1945	Mulberry harbours
1954	First nuclear power		
		1955	Modern circulating pump
1956	Silicon transistor		
		1959	CPM/PERT used
		1960	Sydney Opera House
1961	Person in space	1961	Systems building
1969	Person on moon		
1974	Oil crisis		
	Personal computer		
		1980	Intelligent building postulated
1983	First IBM PC	1983	Property boom starts

However, the significant changes that have given us the technology that we know today occurred during the so-called scientific revolution which took place in Western Europe in the seventeenth century. What was important in this revolution was not the creation of an array of new artefacts but a new way of thinking about the world. Such powerful figures as Francis Bacon (1561–1626) were striving to find a new order to the world and a dominion over nature. This period saw the rise of a mechanistic view of nature in the works of philosophers like Descartes (1596–1650) which offered a new certainty about the world and a rational control over nature, society and the individual. During the period that followed, known as the Age of Reason or the Enlightenment, the dilemma about the benefits and problems of technology was much argued about. The impact of this new order and thinking gave rise to the industrial revolution in the eighteenth and nineteenth centuries. This saw the invention and development of a series of machines that transformed energy to undertake work and also heralded the change from a feudal, agrarian society to the urbanized, capitalist society that makes up the developed world. It is important to realize that these technological changes were occurring at the same time as a series of social and political revolutions throughout Europe in which new power groupings were endeavouring to take control. Technology was a part of these changes and not some external influence on them.

During these times of change, technology was by no means seen universally as a good thing. The Luddites (1811–1816) destroyed machinery invented to displace their labour. Their arrest and subsequent execution starkly demonstrate the conflict in perceptions about the value of technology.[1] As well as opposition from those directly affected by technology in the early nineteenth century, there was an intellectual and aesthetic opposition which saw a new romantic movement with a focus on an idealized rural beauty characterized in the work of the poet Wordsworth and the paintings of Constable. Such romanticisms survived through the nineteenth century in the arts and crafts movement which abhorred technological production and favoured craft labour.

In the last hundred years, technology has been subsumed totally into the social framework of the developed world which lives with the advent of electricity, cars, aeroplanes, nuclear power and space exploration. Within the last 20 years, the rise of computers and biotechnology have stimulated new ideas about 'man's dominion over nature' and predictions of a further social and industrial revolution.

WORKPIECE 3.1

PROBLEMATIC IMPACTS

Technological impacts can be good or bad, depending on your moral values and who you are.

Identify three technologies associated with the building and development industries which have been the subject of conflict: locally, nationally and globally.

Consider the positions taken about these three

technologies by:

- a site manager;
- a site labourer;
- a design professional.

State what you think about each of the technologies.

TECHNOLOGY ASSESSMENT

If technology is so bound up in the way we think and our everyday lives, how do we assess its impact? What are the criteria? How can we establish a critical framework for understanding relationships between technology and the environment? Technology assessment (TA) is one approach.

This is a rational process for determining and evaluating the impact of technology. It emphasizes those consequences that are unintended, indirect or delayed. It has its roots in the counter culture of the 1960s which had seen such apocalyptic popular novels as Rachael Carson's *Silent Spring*, scientific world studies like the Club of Rome's *The Limits to Growth*[2], and the horrors that the military–industrial complex could impose on Vietnam. The message from these to the public was that technology was out of control: short-term rewards were achieved by a powerful few, whereas large numbers suffered consequences and the world was being systematically destroyed in the long term.

TA was formalized in the USA with an Office of Technology Assessment, but in the UK such activities were left to Royal Commissions. The formal institutional backing for technology assessment in America meant that much of the methodological work comes from there.[3,4] These works do, however, provide us with a framework to meet our objectives here. Similar ideas have arisen in the last five years in the field of environmental impact assessment for evaluating the development of large construction and industrial projects[5], environmental management systems[6] and environmental assessment of buildings.[7]

Technology assessment can be applied after the introduction of technology or before. In the latter case, it can provide information for policy makers and designers. In the former, it is more academic, being concerned to understand the consequences of change. The process of TA involves undertaking 10 activities shown in Table 3.2.[4] These are not performed sequentially but will be used iteratively to build up a detailed picture of the assessment required.

Table 3.2 Components of a technology assessment[4]

1.	Problem definition:	bounding the extent of the enquiry.
2.	Technological description:	the important technical parameters and how the technology is delivered.
3.	Technological forecast:	the character and timing of potential technological changes.
4.	Social description:	the individuals and groups involved or displaced by the technology and its delivery systems.
5.	Social forecast:	the character and timing of potential social and political changes.
6.	Impact identification:	determining the direct and higher order effects.
7.	Impact analysis:	determining the magnitude and seriousness of the effects.
8.	Impact evaluation:	considering the interrelationship and significance relative to the societal goals and objectives.
9.	Policy analysis:	comparing options and looking at the longer term implications on political structure.
10.	Communication of results.	

Such a study can involve a large amount of effort, resources and time. It is also fundamentally interdisciplinary. Of particular interest is the determination of impacts. Direct impacts are those effects that are directly attributable to the technology. Higher order impacts are those attributable to the products of the direct effects or indirect effects, thus, effects are involved in a chain reaction from the direct through the various levels of higher order impacts.

You can undertake a non-rigorous technology assessment by using Table 3.3 to help you think through the impacts of a particular technology. In this matrix the columns represent the areas of effect, namely on the environment, personally, organizationally, socially and economically. These effects can be remembered through the mnemonic EPOSE. The rows represent various distances from the direct effects, both spatially and in time. In using the table it is important to identify the involvement within each area of impact, in particular the people and groups who will benefit and suffer from the technology. An example for air-conditioning is shown in Table 3.4.

Table 3.3 Technological Impact Analysis

	Environmental spatial, aesthetic, resources, pollution	Personal physiological, psychological	Organizational companies, authorities, political parties, formal groups	Social families, cultures, informal groups	Economic investment, return or reward
List Involvement e.g. Users, extractors, manufacturers, distributors, etc.					
Direct Impact					
2nd Order Same time, different place					
3rd Order Immediate future, same place					
4th Order Immediate future, different place					
5th Order Long future					

Table 3.4 Technological Impact Analysis

	Environmental spatial, aesthetic, resources, pollution	*Personal* physiological, psychological	*Organizational* companies, authorities, political parties, formal groups	*Social* families, cultures, informal groups	*Economic* investment, return or reward
List Involvement e.g. Users, extractors, manufacturers, distributors, etc.	Building itself Local environment Materials for equipment Energy Refrigerant	Building users Local residents Families of building users Manufacturers Installers Maintenance	Resident organization Building owner Manufacturer Installer Maintenance	Work group Family group	Capital cost Running cost
Direct Impact	Space reduction in building Sight of external cooling towers and air grills	Fixed indoor environment Change in building form Increased employment		Broke up old work groups	Running cost Improved productivity Reduction in net lettable area Increase in rent available
2nd Order Same time, different place	Pollution from power station	Legionnaires' disease Changed expectations			
3rd Order Immediate future, same place		Sick building syndrome	Allowed larger organizations Allowed office technology	Centralization of offices More parents working away from home	
4th Order Immediate future, different place					
5th Order Long future	Resource depletion materials, energy CFC damage Acid rain	Reduced quality of environment causes distress and illness	Office as machine	Change social structure in offices through different office design	

Common descriptions of technology tend only to consider its direct position and effects. This is because people who advocate the case of a particular technology can usually only see the benefits. It is the higher order impacts which normally reveal the negative effects on something or someone. Clearly if you set the boundaries of such a study narrow enough, you can avoid seeing many negative problems; however, they do still exist. In the past, governments have tried to aggregate the costs and benefits of all the impacts by placing a money value on them, e.g. in motorway or nuclear power station inquiries. This has great problems because of trying to put financial worth on personal values and so different individuals and groups see the same impacts with different costs and benefits.

WORKPIECE 3.2

IMPACT ASSESSMENT

Use the Impact Assessment sheet to analyse the following technologies:

1. Asbestos panelling
2. Robotic brick laying machine
3. Microporous paint
4. A learning control system for lights
5. Low energy lights.

In a group discussion try to determine a consensus on the continuing use of these technologies.

THE DEVELOPMENT AND APPLICATION OF TECHNOLOGY

Why is there so much argument about the sources of technological change? How far have changes in society impinged on or been reflected by changes in technology? Prior to the Industrial Revolution, technology was developed close to its point of application by the people who used it and also benefited from it. Following the Industrial Revolution, particularly in the last 60 years, the development of technology has often been undertaken away from the point of use, by people trained to develop technology, to be used by people who will not benefit directly from it. In the section on history, we showed that technological change and social change go hand in hand. In this section, we will show that impacts are tied to technological development and application in a reciprocal way.[8]

We, as the public, are seldom aware when choices in the development and application of technology arise. The 'technological imperative'[9] suggests that specific technological objectives (for example, higher buildings, better roads, tighter environmental control) become dominant policy concerns in place of directly providing for people's needs. This arises because there are major self-interests that are now supported by technological growth in the form of the technical elite, a large technological product industry and a political system that needs quick fixes. The result is that the technological imperative becomes automatic and western industrial society develops a total dependence on technology.[9] Such a process does not just select the technological approach; it also, in the process of 'reverse adaptation'; often redirects the objectives of the development.[10] Thus, for example, building design becomes concerned with the integration of building services plant rather than the comfort of the building's users. Decisions are made to optimize the means without regard to the original ends. How can we overcome this or reverse the process?

It is useful to make a separation between 'active' and 'passive' approaches to technological design in buildings. (These are sometimes referred to as selective and adaptive approaches.) **Active solutions** involve the use of high technology which is added to a building to provide for a particular need; for instance, lights are added to illuminate tasks. Active solutions tend to be only attached to the building so that they can be easily replaced or adapted to match the need better. However, they tend to use high grade energy, are vulnerable to failure and require maintenance support. **Passive solutions** use technological thinking to develop the whole building design to provide for the needs. In the example above, a building can be designed to be daylighted through design of its form and envelope. Passive solutions are not flexible and can only be modified by major redevelopment. However, they are not dependent on energy so are not vulnerable and are sustainable, requiring little maintenance.

It is important to understand the notion of **'technical fix'** in the development of technology as this is also a derivative of the technological imperative. A technical solution is found to a problem; for example, air-conditioning to prevent overheating in offices. The solution causes its own problems (i.e. higher order impacts) and these problems are solved by more technology; such solutions are called technical fixes. In the case of air-conditioning, the use of wet cooling towers in air-conditioning systems has been directly linked to outbreaks of legionnaires' disease. The solution is to put a biocide into the cooling water; in turn the biocide may corrode pipework and so further technological solutions in the way of corrosion inhibiting additives may be necessary. Thus, the technological imperative may cause a cascade of technical fixes. The provisions for the technical fixes may be more costly than the original solution and may significantly reduce its effectiveness. The radical approach would be to remove the need for air-conditioning in the first place!

THE IMPACT ON IDEAS

As we have mentioned technology not only delivers artefacts but also influences ideas and ways of thinking about problems. This influence extends to aspects which would be regarded as non-technological, such as the architectural aesthetic and the approach to building functions.

The impact of the intellectual scientism in the eighteenth century created a drive for rationality and design which was met by a return to classicism using its clear roles and principles.[11] There was also a move for secular buildings to achieve grandeur and monumental scale that demonstrated the new human power over nature. At the same time, technical rationalism spawned a need to accommodate the new institutional bureaucracies, particularly in post-revolutionary France. In many ways, this thinking of the eighteenth century spread into the rational planning of cities in the nineteenth century which logically forced the provision of water supplies, sewage systems and public spaces. In a more humanistic way, technical rationality gave rise to utilitarianism which initiated urban social housing and latterly model towns and garden cities. Such initiatives were a set of technical fixes as a result of the technological impact from urban factories spewing pollution, noise and ugliness and forcing cramped conditions. The technology of rail transport made the idea of a garden city a reality by allowing workers to live away from urban factories and rural towns; rail travel, in turn, has caused another set of problems.

The success of technology in supplying institutional and individual rewards at the start of the twentieth century saw it taking over as the power behind ideas. The modern movement in architecture through the work of Behrens (1868–1940), Gropius (1883–1969), Mies van der Rohe (1886–1969) and Le Corbusier (1887–1966) saw buildings as machines which could then be simplified and optimized, which could display an honesty of form, and which could involve standardized construction. These modernists were socially orientated but through their rational professional élite sought to build Utopias for people. In a dramatic way the modern movement has influenced both the style of buildings and the development of technology for buildings even to the present day. High-rise housing and brutalist public buildings became the symbols of the late 1950s and 1960s. Such technological developments, which enabled the creative use of reinforced concrete and the realization of prefabricated systems buildings, were major advances. However, the failure of these buildings constructionally, environmentally and socially must also be attributed directly to the impact of technological thinking.

Technological thinking did not stop with the demise of the modern movement, but has been reformed in the high tech style of building. Such buildings as Richard Rogers' Lloyds of London and Norman Foster's Sainsbury Centre have drawn on aircraft technology and used structural glasses to provide a different modern statement. Again, there is a desire for honesty both in the structure and the services, with these being exposed. Again, conceptions have come from technology and, reciprocally, technology has been developed to meet the needs of the concept. However, the higher order impacts are seldom assessed.

Why have we taken such an abstract look at technology? This was necessary to challenge how we think about technology and to establish a framework for evaluating its impact. Now we focus on the impact of hard physical products of technology and consider components, materials and functional design. Technology has delivered new products, with new properties, which has enabled buildings to be constructed in different ways, faster and cheaper, and for new characteristics to be given

IMPACT ON PRODUCTS AND FUNCTIONAL DESIGN

Figure 3.1 Sainsbury Centre, University of East Anglia, showing use of glass and steel. Designed by Foster Associates. (Tom Muir.)

to buildings. The ability to think in a logical way and to calculate consequences has also led to an ability to design things in abstract rather than through a process of trial and error. These impacts have been so significant that we will consider just three: high-rise buildings, air-conditioning and intelligent buildings.

HIGH-RISE STRUCTURES AND LIFTS

At the end of the nineteenth century high-rise buildings became a feature of the downtown business areas of cities like Chicago. Why did this happen? What generated the new structural forms? Part of the answer lies in the advent of the steel frame which facilitated the development of tall office buildings. Clearly, socio-economic needs such as high land costs and demand for space were also factors. Iron frames had been used for bridges, factories and warehouses from the early years of the nineteenth century. The materials and the systems for their delivery were already established, as was the structural design expertise. However, it required the development of steel with good tensile properties to construct continuous structural frames which could be made to span greater distances and to rise to greater heights.

Such high buildings required people to climb large numbers of stairs, which consumed time and effort. A solution that occurred

Figure 3.2 Decorative nineteenth century lift shaft, Majolica House, Vienna. Design by Otto Wagner. (Tom Muir.)

simultaneously with the development of the steel frame was the invention of the passenger lift. Again, steam-driven hoists had been used in factories for many years; however, these were considered unsafe due to the danger of ropes breaking. The invention of the safety lift by Elisha Otis in 1854, incorporated a feature that would arrest the lift platform if the rope broke. This encouraged greater public acceptance.[12] A series of further technical developments in wire ropes, electric motors, traction design and automatic controls resulted in the devices we see today.

It is tempting to say that the lift caused high-rise buildings, but it was socio-economic and other technical developments that conspired to make multi-storeys an economic success. Whether for shops or offices, successful high-rise buildings drew people to them in large numbers. Thus, they are clearly manifestations of cities as centres of commerce and transport systems. Indeed another factor in the metamorphosis of downtown business areas was the advance of railways.

The advent of the steel frame caused a standardization in the form, height and depth of buildings. Clearly it is a more energy and resource intensive technology than building low-rise. How can this be balanced against the environmental value of the land? The impact of high-rise construction on social and individual issues is impossible to disaggregate from general changes in society. It is interesting to note current health advice which suggests that people should walk and not take lifts for short journeys.

AIR-CONDITIONING

What other changes have influenced the way we think about and design buildings? High-rise buildings came about for a range of reasons and in turn they generated new demands on the services within buildings. Air-conditioning was one of the results but, like most technologies, there were many years of development of other technologies which eventually allowed for an effective ability to control the temperature and humidity of air in a building in the 1920s.

Mechanical ventilation had been developed in the mining industry about 150 years earlier. This provided a stimulus for the design of fans and an understanding of airflow in ducts. Ventilation was needed in Victorian buildings that were lit by gas lamps to remove combustion products and heat and, as we shall see, one of the needs for air-conditioning is to remove the heat generated by artificial lighting.

Mechanical refrigeration was first developed on a commercial scale to produce artificial ice in 1848. Previously, ice had been cut in the winter and stored. Indeed, early cooling systems in buildings used ice, placed in ventilation ducts, as the source of cold. The uses of refrigeration were mainly for food preservation in ships and for controlling conditions in industrial processes. These early machines used ether as the refrigerant but this was soon superseded by ammonia and latterly in 1931 by freon.[13]

What were the problems in developing of air-conditioning? The ability to control humidity was set out in a patent by Carrier in 1906 in which he solved the complication of controlling temperature and water content of the air at the same time. Air-conditioning was first used in department stores, theatres and cinemas, particularly in the USA where high summer temperatures and humidities made buildings oppressive.

The first fully air-conditioned office was the Millam building in San Antonio, Texas, in 1928. In urban environments, air-conditioning became a solution to environmental control because of having windows closed to eliminate smoke smuts, dust and noise.[14] In a curious way, then, air-conditioning was required because of the various industrial processes that eventually led to its invention.

Although air-conditioning delivered the required environmental conditions, this was at a cost of internal space. In commercial developments the consumption of floor space by ductwork and plant rooms reduced the amount of net lettable area and so made the development less economic. The solution to this required higher velocity air distribution in ducts, more comfortable air distribution in rooms and more efficient plant which could be smaller. Real progress was not achieved until after the second world war by a new technical development in the field of lighting. The fluorescent tube was introduced in 1938 by GEC and Westinghouse. It was the reduced heat output from such lamps, compared with incandescent lamps which reduced the cooling load to a level that could be met by economically sized air-conditioning systems.

It was at this point, after the second world war, that air-conditioning could be used extensively and economically. Further, the USA real estate industry was seeking to enhance its profits with a more rationally planned building centred not on ambient light, ventilation and cooling but on a totally controlled artificial environment. At the same time, the modernist architects were in the ascendant and their skyscraper dreams in a starkly rectangular aesthetic found economic and cultural favour.[14] These technologies enabled a change from a narrow plan re-entrant format of building, which brought light and air to the centre of the block, to a full floor rectangular plan which could more easily be sub-divided and controlled despite larger numbers of staff. These were lit with permanent supplementary artificial lighting and air-conditioned throughout.

In recent years there have been a number of adverse pressures on the use of air-conditioning in buildings. These include the high energy use, the pollution of the external environment and the association of air-conditioning with sick building syndrome. Air-conditioned offices use double the amount of electricity compared with naturally ventilated offices. This is obviously a large recurring cost to the organization that operates the building and also a major depletion of energy resources. Also associated with the use of fossil fuel energy is pollution in the form of greenhouse gases and a contribution to acid rain.

OTHER DISADVANTAGES OF AIR-CONDITIONING

Air-conditioning systems have a direct impact on the environment through the use of chlorofluorocarbons as refrigerants. These leak into the atmosphere during the manufacture, operation and dismantling of refrigerant systems. CFCs are the major cause of destruction of the ozone layer in the atmosphere and are soon to be proscribed under the Montreal protocol. A technological fix in the form of a non-ozone depleting refrigerant is being sought by manufacturers. However, in the interim, refrigerants with low ozone depletion potential are to be used in new equipment but these refrigerants are less efficient and may therefore contribute to higher energy use. Another interim solution is the provision of automatic CFC leak detection equipment and for the provision of pump-down containers to hold CFCs during routine servicing.

As well as environmental problems from CFCs, air-conditioning systems have been shown to breed and spread legionnaires' disease. This disease grows in the wet cooling towers of air-conditioning systems where water is sprayed at temperatures just above ambient temperature, providing ideal growing conditions. Current solutions involve the use of biocides in the cooling water or the use of dry cooling towers. The latter are less efficient and so more energy and more space is required to run the system.

A current radical solution is to eliminate air-conditioning from office buildings in temperate climates. The solution to this problem lies in handling the internal heat gains as the external solar gains can be controlled by good building design. Internal heat gains have increased in recent years due to the introduction of information technology equipment, particularly video display units (VDUs). It is proposed in the next set of building regulations in the UK that designers will have to justify the use of air-conditioning in all buildings. Thus, there will be an impetus to avoid such problems.

INTELLIGENT BUILDINGS

What are intelligent buildings? What kind of impact will they have on designers, developers and builders? This concept has arisen alongside the phenomenal advance of microelectronics, computers and associated technology. Although generally associated with office buildings, the idea has also been applied to retail premises and houses. In some respects an extreme form of intelligent building is the lunar module where the environment was totally controlled by a series of computers and advanced technological systems.

Many aspects of intelligent buildings were around as ideas before the physical realization of practical systems. The initial use of the expression referred to the control of the building services: heating, ventilation and air-conditioning (HVAC), lighting, lifts, fire alarms, fire protection, access, security and electric power. It was proposed that a single computer could integrate the control of all these facilities. This would make them more efficient in energy use and running costs, by delivering an optimum service through more extensive monitoring, and running systems from a single point. Later a building management and maintenance function was postulated which could detect failures in equipment, predict maintenance needs, control stocks of spares and issue job sheets for work to be undertaken.

At the same time as computers were changing the development of building and building services management systems, they were influencing separately the operation of organizations in the building. There were two related areas of influence: office automation and telecommunications.

Office automation centres around the computerization of information generation, storage and processing. It embraces word processing, electronic diaries, databases, desktop publishing, schedule planning, stock control, job control and costing. It has been stimulated by the advent of the powerful and cheap microcomputer which it is possible to supply to nearly all employees.

Telecommunications allows the transfer of information as an input to the office automation system and to employees. The communications can be by voice, fax, electronic mail, graphics and video. The realization of this communication has been due to the ability to digitize information, and to transmit it rapidly through copper cables, fibre optics, microwaves and terrestial and satellite radio.

How do these forms of building intelligence influence building design? What sort of space has had to be found for the extra equipment, some of which has needed special rooms in particular locations? The heat emitted by the equipment has forced a rethink about the scale and operation of environmental control systems. Service ducts have had to be enlarged to accommodate the extra cabling and methods have had to be devised to lead these cables to workstations.

Unfortunately, intelligent buildings based on technical systems have not been wholly successful in delivering such a grand notion of total control. Although most technology can be made to work, given enough money, it is the continuing reliable and effective operation that is important. The reasons for failures were technical deficiencies in the systems, an inability of systems to work together, and inappropriate design of systems such that they did not provide what organizations and people need in their building. This has caused a rethink about the definition of intelligent buildings: it is not what they have in the way of facilities, but what they can do for an organization that is important. What they can do is facilitate good management and operations of both the building and the organization.[15] The functional side of management requires good communications, information gathering, and decision making and the human side of management requires that people are healthy and motivated. When an intelligent building assists these management activities, then real value is added to the building. Information technology is a necessary part of an intelligent building but it is not sufficient in itself to produce an intelligent building.

In the last section we described the development and impact of a number of technologies which radically changed buildings. But what about the impact of technology on the process of designing, constructing and operating buildings? The objectives behind most of these technologies is to speed up the process of procurement and to make the process cheaper. As in the last section, there have been a large number of these technologies and we can only consider a few. There are two sorts of intervention: firstly, where the physical actions are changed by a technology; and secondly, where the management of the process is changed by the technology.

In the first case, an early example is mechanical digging which was used originally in railroad excavation in the USA at the end of the nineteenth century. Previously all digging and earth-moving had to be done by hand, which was time-comsuming and also involved large numbers of itinerant and undisciplined labourers. Clearly such equipment could be seen as removing much of the drudgery and backbreaking work; however, the rewards were not received by the displaced labour – indeed they were unable to obtain work. We shall look at one such new technology, computer aided draughting/design, which is revolutionizing design and draughting.

In the second case we shall look at operational research which has allowed tighter control over the processes of design, construction and operation. As has been pointed out before in this chapter, these developments are not isolated but are taking place at the same time as each other and other organizational changes, thus it is not possible to provide a one-dimensional cause-and-effect story.

WORKPIECE 3.3

TECHNOLOGICAL CHANGES

List three important new technological changes you are aware of. Discuss how these will affect:

- building design;
- the construction process;

in 5 years' time and in 10 years' time.

COMPUTER AIDED DESIGN/DRAUGHTING (CAD)

The 'D' in CAD has two meanings: design and draughting. The former concerns the development of the concepts of building design on a computer; the latter involves the preparation of drawings for building production from already developed building designs. CAD allows the rapid creation, editing and manipulation of a wide variety of basic shapes. (Designing on paper resulted in a great amount of redrawing, or erasing and redrawing, as the design developed. This is considered wasteful in time and effort as it breaks the design flow or increases the production task.)

Further advantages, particularly for draughting, include the availability of libraries of details which allow standard forms to be incorporated easily or repetitive elements to be transferred throughout the design. On the design side, visualization of the design in three dimensions should allow a better understanding of the design by the designer and an easier and fuller ability to communicate the design to other team members, clients and users.

The impact on design has not yet been dramatic as the majority of designers still think through paper sketches. At the moment, CAD is used mainly to provide perspective visualizations or for production drawings. For less creative and more standardized designs such as houses and industrial sheds, then CAD is a direct link between design and draughting which provides the productivity improvement. The fuller realization of CA Design as a creative tool requires both a change in skills and thinking on the part of designers, and the availability of better software. Currently computers are very good at representing solid-line geometric forms, particularly rectangles, but they are less successful at representing a fuzzy concept, where solidity of line is not desirable as it fixes the thinking of the designer. Once the designer feels satisfied with the concept, the computer needs to be able to solidify the design from a series of fuzzy images into a coordinate mapped drawing which can be used as the basis of draughting. This requires considerably more complicated software than straight art drawing packages or straight draughting packages. A worrying impact of CAD, then, is that it will force a standardization of design around geometric figures that the computer can produce rather than liberate the designer's creativity in a more productive way.

The impact on draughting has been more significant, mainly in the form of productivity gains. The greater the degree of standardization or repetition in detailing, the greater the benefits. Software and hardware are sold heavily with a number of great promises of accuracy, transferrability, changeability and presentability, all of which will improve productivity and reduce the number of errors in the total design. Thus, these impacts on draughting have meant a reduction in the need for technicians, but the type of technician required has also changed: they now require the skills to operate the hardware and software. This has created a new problem of skill shortage and a heavy reliance on the person who can operate the machine. The system is therefore vulnerable to the loss of skilled staff and also to the breakdown of the equipment. To overcome the personnel problems, new technological development has been directed at 'de-skilling' the computer operation so that people with only limited skills are required.

A more negative impact of computer technology has been the increase in illnesses associated with their use. These include eye strain, a number of skin complaints and repetitive strain injury from the continuous input of data through computer keyboards.

Other technical developments centre around the integration of other computer functions with the CAD software. These include design calculations and simulations, the preparation of bills of quantity, the automatic issuing of workshop drawings or even compiling instructions for computer controlled machines, and the support of the operations and maintenance function of building use. Each of these will have direct impacts which are impressive; however, in your careers you will be able to observe how the higher order impacts are accommodated or ignored.

What other changes are occurring in technology and the management of the building process? One important development through operational research is critical path analysis.

Operational research is the general term used for a number of scientific planning and simulation techniques used to optimize the operation and management of industries. As the construction industry is project-based (that is, buildings are usually one-off activities), optimization tends to involve the variables of time, cost and quality. In particular, much work has been done on the time planning side through the use of network analysis such as 'critical path analysis'. Such techniques enable very large and complex projects to be controlled so that they can be undertaken on time and to budget.

Critical path analysis (CPA) is a technique devised to schedule a series of activities, some of which can be done simultaneously and some of which need to be completed before others can start. It involves breaking a project down into a set of tasks and then connecting the task with fixed precedence relationships. A time duration has to be provided for each task so that the total time for the project can be calculated using network analysis. From this, activities can be identified which it is critical to undertake if the project is to run to time. These activities do not have any spare time (called 'float' or 'slack') for mistakes or delays and the series of these activities is known as the 'critical path'.

The use of such techniques has improved productivity although the extra personnel and time involved in their use sometimes cannot be justified on smaller projects. It has also meant that organizations and people must work to the programme, which fixes the task breakdown and the method of operation even if there is a better way of doing the job. People become simply cogs in a production machine which has been devised by technical specialists. This has led to a de-skilling of crafts and a disengagment of people from their work, which has been one of the reasons blamed for a decline in quality in the industry. It is important to understand these sorts of technology. The building industry is set to become more competitive and it will rely on the development of new ideas and techniques to promote quality and efficiency.

WORKPIECE 3.4

THE DEVELOPMENT OF APPROPRIATE TECHNOLOGY

Consider the disposal of sewage within a house where you have stayed recently. Do you think that this meets the criteria of an appropriate technology? How do you think it could be improved?

Compare the use of timber and steel for making roof trusses, trying to decide on the one that could meet the criteria for appropriate technology.

High specification office buildings sometimes have marble-clad entrance halls. Consider whether this is an appropriate use of materials.

Is a wind turbine used for generating electricity to heat a house an appropriate technology?

THE NEED FOR APPROPRIATE TECHNOLOGY

Modern society has been dominated and obsessed with technological change and the creation of new 'styles' to go with it. Are there alternatives? Should we be exploring different kinds of technology? How can we establish development and planning policies or design buildings so that they do not require advanced technology at all?

There is a growing awareness of the need to create sustainable environmental policies and ecologically sound buildings. The ideas that are generating this approach are derived from different sources. In the 1960s, E.F. Schumacher wrote a book called *Small is Beautiful* and established an approach to design in the developing world called **intermediate technology.** This has evolved in such a way as to influence developed as well as developing countries.

This chapter makes clear that, although technology has delivered considerable direct benefits, some of the higher order impacts have caused suffering and discontent. Although this analysis has focused on the developed and industrialized countries, many of the negative impacts have been experienced by the developing countries who have had to deliver cheap materials and suffer high pollution risks to make the developed countries rich. At the same time the developing countries have been slipping further behind the income per capita levels of the West and also experiencing major social and environmental catastrophies. Many people considered that the benefits from technology could help the developing countries improve their social and economic position, but much of the direct transfer of technology has resulted in the rich of the developing countries becoming richer and the poor poorer. In an attempt to take benefits directly to the people who needed it most, a number of intermediate or **appropriate technology (AT)** initiatives were made.[16,17] The aims of AT are summarized in Table 3.5.

Table 3.5 Appropriate technology

This aims to:

- improve the quality of life of the people;
- maximize the use of renewable resources;
- create self-sufficiency where people live now.

This should involve:

- employment of local skills;
- use of local materials;
- use of local finances;
- respect for local cultures and practices;
- direct satisfaction of local wishes and needs.

It is clear from the aims of AT that it rejects the primacy of the market economy in favour of a more equitable satisfaction of primary needs. The technological skills developed in the West are not geared to these aims, therefore a new approach to technological development in the developing countries has had to be learned. Work is generally undertaken in the field alongside the beneficiaries of the development; they are part of the work and also help to make it most effective. The development is gradual in order to avoid ecological and social problems and so the results are sustainable. Many projects centre around water supply and sewage treatment which need to be integrated into the whole social infrastructure so that they are respected by all and benefit all.[18]

The slower, more considered nature of AT development has a relevance for the developed countries. Although building developments in the developed countries are not generally associated with primary needs, it is important that a building's long-term worth is understood. The extremes of benefit and suffering that the development and use of technology can bring need to be understood. In fact, the concerns in the developed countries for the ecological environment are beginning to expose some of these issues. However, the economics of technology will direct solutions towards technological fixes rather than to appropriate development. The development of the built environment is a long term social as well as financial investment. Thus, invoking appropriate technology aims – an understanding of the context of development, a considered use of energy and materials, an awareness of the pollution that results and a respect for people – must be critical for the future.[19]

Whilst some of the more exciting and glamorous advances in technology centre on buildings like the Pompidou Centre in Paris, or buildings such as those designed by Future Systems Design which are heavily influenced by aircraft and space age technology, more meaningful technological advances may be found in the application of appropriate technology. An example of a low cost, low energy innovation which could have a significant impact on cities throughout the world is the Parry People Mover designed and built by a small company in the Black Country in England. This system – a form of mini-tram which depends on a flywheel motor charged by low voltage electricity (possibly generated by solar panels) – costs less than a third of the high energy transportation methods that have been introduced in many cities. The higher order impacts have been considered in the design.

WORKPIECE 3.5

MATERIALS AND APPROPRIATE TECHNOLOGY

List the materials that have been used in the construction of the building you live in (your flat or house) under the following headings:

- roof
- walls
- structure
- floors.

Do these materials meet the aims of appropriate technology?

Has the construction of your building met the five criteria that appropriate technology should involve?

How could appropriate technology have been used more?

SUMMARY

In this chapter we have looked at the impact of technology on the built environment. These impacts have occurred both on the practical level and on the ideas behind buildings. We have shown that technological development takes place beside the social and political changes that occur in society, thus impacts are difficult to segregate from general changes. Technological developments have broader impacts than those seen directly. We presented a technique for thinking through the impacts of technology more completely. Often these higher order impacts reveal disadvantages from the use of the technology and these tend to be borne differently by different groups in society. The technological imperative causes change in a particular direction which may hide the higher order impacts. Problematic impacts arising from the use of a technology are often solved by the use of further technologies which may cause a new set of problems; these solutions were called technical fixes. The impacts of a number of technologies on the functional design of buildings and on the process of designing, constructing and operating buildings were described. Although these all had positive direct impacts, they were all shown to have negative impacts as well. Finally, the transfer of technology from the developed countries to the developing countries was considered briefly. The technology from developed countries was shown not to be able to improve the basic needs of the vast majority of people in these countries. The aims of appropriate technology were outlined as a different direction for change which meets the needs of people locally and that this is relevant to the developing and developed countries equally.

KEY CONCEPTS

- Technological impacts can be good and bad depending on the perspectives of different people and on their short and long term duration.
- Technological development and impact are directly connected to changes in social and political issues generally occurring in society.
- Technology causes impacts directly and in higher order effects.
- Impacts concern environmental, personal, organizational, societal and economic issues (use the mnemonic EPOSE).
- Technology has affected ideas behind buildings as well as components and products in buildings.
- Watch for technical fixes, i.e. technical solutions to technological problems which give further problems.
- Appropriate technology seeks to control the direct and higher order impacts so that there is general benefit.

REFERENCES

1. Robins, K. and Webster, F. (1985) Luddism, new technology and the critique of political economy, in *Science, Technology and the Labour Process*, Vol. 2, (eds B. Young and L. Levidow), Free Association Books.
2. Meadows, D.H., Meadows, D.L., Randers, J. and Behrens W.W. (1972) *The Limits to Growth*, Pan.
3. Coates J. (1976) Technology Assessment, the benefits, the costs, the consequences. *The Futurist*, 5 December, pp. 225–331.
4. Porter, A.L., Rossini, F.A., Carpenter, S.R. and Roper, A.T. (1980) *A Guidebook for Technology Assessment and Impact Analysis*, Elsevier, North Holland, New York.
5. Rau, J.G. and Wooten, D.C. (eds) (1980) *Environmental Impact Analysis Handbook*, McGraw-Hill, New York.
6. BS 7750 (1992) *Environmental Management System*, British Standards Institution.

7.   BRE (1990) *Building Research Establishment Environmental Assessment Method; for new offices designs 1/90*, Building Research Establishment, Garston, England.

8.   Boyle, G., Elliot, D. and Roy, R. (1977) *The Politics of Technology*, Open University Press.

9.   Hales, M. (1982) *Science or Society*, Pan.

10. Winner, L. (1977) *Autonomous Technology*, MIT Press, Cambridge, Mass.

11. Frampton, K. (1985) *Modern Architecture, A Critical History*, Thames and Hudson.

12. Strakosch, G.R. (1982) *Vertical Transportation*, Wiley, New York.

13. Billington, N.S. and Roberts, B.M. (1982) *Building Services Engineering*, Pergamon Press.

14. Banham, R. (1984) *The Architecture of the Well Tempered Environment*, 2nd edn, Architecture Press.

15. Boyd, D. (ed.) (1994) *Intelligent Buildings and Management*, Arthur Waller.

16. Schumacher, E.F. (1974) *Small is Beautiful, technology as if people mattered*, Sphere Books.

17. McRobie, G. (1982) *Small is Possible*, Sphere Books.

18. Dunn, P.D. (1978) *Appropriate Technology, technology with a human face*, MacMillan.

19. Ekins, P. (ed.) (1986) *The Living Economy, a new economics in the making*, Routledge and Kegan Paul.

FURTHER READING

Armytage, W.H.G. (1961) *A Social History of Engineering*, Faber.

British Steel (1992) *History of Early Steel*, Architecture Teaching Programme.

Franklin, U. (1992) *The Real World of Technology*, Anansi, Ontario.

Giedon, S. (1948) *Mechanisation Takes Command*, Oxford University Press.

Harvie, C., Martin, G. and Scharf, A. (1970) *Industrialisation and Culture 1830–1914*, MacMillan for Open University Press.

Hellman, L. (1986) *Architecture for Beginners*, Writers and Readers.

MacKenzie, D. and Wacjman, J. (1985) *The Social Shaping of Technology: how the refrigerator got its hum*, Open University Press.

Mesthene, E.G. (1970) *Technological Change: its impact on Man and Society*, Harvard University Press, Mass.

PART TWO

THE
PROCESS OF
DEVELOPMENT

BUILDING TOGETHER

DAVID CHAPMAN

Are there fundamental factors which influence the way people relate to each other and to the land? How are these shown in the way buildings and spaces relate to one another: is it in the form of individual buildings, clusters or groups of buildings, or in towns or in villages? What are the social, spiritual, political and economic forces which interact with the forces of nature to shape the pattern and form of settlement?

This chapter looks at the ways people tackle these issues, the relationships between social organizations and natural environments and the varied built environments which can result.

After studying this chapter you should be able to:

● identify and distinguish environmental factors which influence the relationships between buildings and the spaces between them;

● understand ways different cultures, human aspirations and interventions have shaped the development of places in the past, and how they continue to do so today;

● appreciate qualities of places and the spaces between buildings;

● study places, to assess their qualities and to consider how they may be improved.

69

INTRODUCTION

It has been claimed that the built environment is 'a political system in its own right'.[1] The relationships between buildings and the spaces they shape exert powerful pressures upon the users of places and what they can and cannot do.

The physical form of the places we use today has been developed and adapted, often over many centuries, to respond to the needs and aspirations of each period, and also to take advantage of the natural benefits which could be gained from the prevailing climatic and geographical conditions of the area.

The cumulative effects of many individual actions over long periods, such as constructing a new building, building a new road, blocking, an old path, joining a procession, all fundamentally influence the quality and usability of the resultant built environments. When we recognize this we inevitably wish to understand more about the forces that shape our built environment, the processes of change, the qualities of equitable and enjoyable places, and some of the ways we can help to create them.

The variety of factors that influence the processes of change is great and the relationships between them are changing through time, but despite this a high degree of stability also exists. An example of the relationship between dynamic processes of change and the superficial appearance of stability is given by some cloud formations which look solid and stable but are in fact a maelstrom of change within.

COMPLEXITY AND UNCERTAINTY

Though for many of us our daily lives give the feeling and impression of stability and security, for others it is far from so. Climatic changes and natural forces continue to reshape the surface of the planet upon which we live. Global climatic changes, in particular global warming, have become of crucial interest and research. Tidal erosion and wind erosion are obvious examples, but less obvious and continual changes may be occurring.

Changes in the social, political and spiritual systems of places occur both gradually and, sometimes, dramatically. In their most extreme form these changes can result from open war between groups of competing interests or beliefs. In more subtle but no less profound ways societies are continuously changing in both composition, for instance where people move into or out of an area, and in ethos, for example where a religious belief grows or declines. Economic values and systems can also apparently change quite quickly, for instance with the rapid decline of the power of communism in Eastern Europe and the ascendancy of capitalism in parts of the western world.

These changes, whether natural, social or economic, are potentially complex and uncertain. Nevertheless there are perhaps some vague patterns or tendencies that we can observe and study, which might inform our behaviour and decision-making and might 'incline' society, and the pattern of development we create, towards a safer, more equitable and more robust future.

A multitude of individual decisions shape the character of development and the nature of change. Within any society decisions are continuously being made about future investments involving human, physical or financial resources. These decisions may be made at a very local level or be controlled and influenced by powerful people or organizations on a regional, national or international scale. While every individual decision or action contributes to the ultimate quality and form of our settlements, it is important to recognize that individuals and institutions often have a powerful control or at least influence upon decision-making and consequently upon the shape and content of places.

It is perhaps useful to draw a distinction between the processes of change in established settlements and the factors which may influence the creation of a new settlement. In existing settlements change may be predominantly incremental and evolutionary, although there may be large-scale changes in areas of redevelopment or urban 'degeneration' and regeneration. At various times and places it has been decided to plan and develop completely new or substantially expanded settlements. In these cases, which are still occurring in many parts of the world and include the Urban Village movement in Britain, a vision or concept is combined with organizing principles and criteria for the whole development.

It is useful to consider the different forces at work and the advantages and disadvantages of incremental or 'revolutionary' change.

Although we are unlikely to be able to understand all of the forces at work in the formation of the built environment, or to be able to control them, it may be possible to exercise some influence upon the processes of change. The more we understand about the forces and diverse agents of change, having both direct and indirect effect [2], the more likely we are to be able to manage and influence decisions and the resultant built environments. Understanding some of the processes of change, however, is not enough. It is equally important that we try to understand the qualities and characteristics that make places good and enjoyable to be in.

UNDERSTANDING INFLUENCE

THE INFLUENCE OF
NATURE

LOCATION

Fundamental to the development of settlements, and thus the relation-ships between buildings, are the factors relating to location. Clearly global position, in both latitude and longitude, determines broad cli-matic conditions. Local geographical conditions further shape the immediate microclimate and thus inform decision-making for both indi-vidual buildings and groups of buildings. Despite widely different cli-matic conditions across the world, and throughout the seasons of the year, human needs are broadly similar. We need to avoid the extremes of temperature and to have shelter from wind, rain and snow. In some lat-itudes the latter is not very difficult and sunlight is a welcome pleasure, warming bodies and lighting homes, but in other areas the creation of shade and keeping cool is highly desirable. These factors not only influ-ence the design of individual buildings but also have an important effect upon the relationships between buildings. In places like Valletta and Medina in Malta the tall buildings enclosing narrow streets create deep shade and encourage air currents to cool them, while in more northern towns streets are often wider to allow sun to penetrate between the buildings.

CLIMATE

The extremes of our global climate are completely inhospitable and yet human intervention can make habitable environments in both equator-ial heat and polar cold. We all understand the ingredients of climate and how to dress to be most comfortable, and we soon change clothes if the weather changes. So do building designs and groupings. A building which fails to respond to climatic influences is as inappropriate as some-one in an overcoat lying on a hot beach. The ingredients of climatic interaction are complex and can produce almost limitless variations in local conditions. Our climate is created by changes in the earth's atmos-pheric pressure as influenced by the planet's topography and hydrology and particularly the effect of solar energy, thus influencing:

- insulation and the earth – 'heat budget';
- atmospheric moisture – humidity and precipitation;
- atmospheric motion – winds and storms.

Approaches to building construction and the form of buildings and set-tlements enable us to modify our environment and to make it both liveable and civilized. Two important building elements which visually indicate climatic influences are roofs and windows.

In wet climates pitched roofs are the easiest way of directing rain off the building, and where snow is prevalent they are more steeply pitched to shed the snow load. In hotter and drier climates flat roofs are used partly because water penetration is not a major problem, but also because they can collect precious water into cisterns or containers below the building.

Windows in hot sunny climates are small but deeply recessed to keep the interior of buildings cool. In temperate climates windows can give good light inside.

Thick walls are found in both hot and cold climates because their thermal mass helps to modify the extremes of temperature variation.

WORKPIECE 4.1

EXPLORING LOCATIONAL AND CLIMATIC INFLUENCES ON SETTLEMENT PATTERN AND FORM

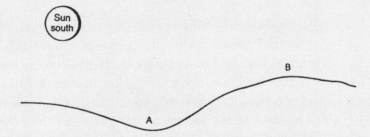

Make a list, and annotate the section above, of the kinds of factor which might influence the design and layout of a settlement at points A and B. Assume that the climate is similar to the one where you live, then try the exercise again for an imaginary climate quite opposite to your own.

UNDERLYING GEOLOGY

The geological characteristics of an area influence the pattern and character of settlement. The location of desired minerals has influenced settlement locations, for example lead mining towns in Derbyshire and coal mining villages in Scotland, Wales and northern England. The availability of natural materials (stone, timber and clay) exerts a strong influence upon the construction and appearance of buildings. Underlying geology is inextricably connected with the topography and hydrology of an area. The relative positions and hardness of rock formations influence the landform and landscape characteristics. Surface water run-off, drainage and watercourses respond to the topographical form and also help to create it.

VARIATIONS ACROSS THE GLOBE

The variations of climate and location of places in which we as a human race seek to build are evidently very wide. By observing traditional patterns and methods of building we can discover various ways in which favourable conditions have been created for human use. Understanding the variety of environmental factors that influence the design of buildings and settlements across the globe is very important.

The transference of building form and technologies from one place to another can be problematic and requires careful consideration. The 'international style' of architecture might be considered to have been fundamentally flawed by this simple point. The stylistic approach implied building forms and characteristics which were to be used worldwide; for example, flat roofs which performed poorly in wet climates, and large expanses of glazing in hot climates, requiring blinds and shades to control solar heat gain. Relationships between buildings tended to be handled in the same way with buildings separated in landscaped settings in hot and cold climates, losing both the natural 'air-conditioning' in the former, and the 'urbanity' of the latter.

HUMAN INTERVENTION

Relationships between people are inevitably complex and vary through time and history. Individual interests, family interests, tribal interests and the interests of mixed societies often create tensions and pressures. At their extremes these can result in open hostility and warfare. Even in superficially stable societies, tension and discrimination can exist. The state of the society at any place and time clearly affects the patterns of development and the relationships between buildings. The locations of many early settlements were clearly influenced by the imperative for defence. Sites on hill tops or surrounded by a river's meander were favoured positions and the shape of towns responded to the landform and seized every defensive opportunity. In the late twentieth century our towns and cities world-wide are being influenced by the desire for personal security and avoidance of crime against people and property. This is shaping the approach to the layout of buildings and the relationships between them, as well as the designs of individual buildings.

CASE STUDY – WEST STOWE, SUFFOLK

All that we know of prehistoric West Stowe comes from archaeological investigations, and yet there is evidence of successive inhabitation stretching over thousands of years.

The area in the Lark valley has one of the greatest concentrations of ancient settlements in East Anglia. The area was perhaps selected because of its position near the river, where a slight hill and light easily cultivated soil gave freedom from flooding and good conditions for crops.

Several periods of use or settlement have been identified with other intervening periods when no evidence of settlement has been found:

- Neolithic people camped on the low hill, made flint tools and hunted in the area at around 8000 BC.
- Neolithic people cleared the woodlands to create fields and a late Neolithic noble was buried in a round barrow there around 2000 BC.
- A farm existed here during the Iron Age *ca.* 200 BC. The 'new' Iron Age technology increased the rate of woodland clearance for farming in the area. Excavation indicates that circular huts were grouped in ditched enclosures at this time.
- During the Romano–British period, the area was used as a pottery and for kilns (between AD 80 and 140).
- An Anglo-Saxon settlement existed on the site from about AD 420 to 650 when the area was gradually absorbed from a new site further east. The Anglo-Saxon farmers lived in three or four family groups of houses, and with a hall as a community building.

Since that time there is little evidence of settlements, except of some mediaeval farming around 1300. Overgrazing and wind erosion made the heather unstable and gave the character to the Breckland heaths that exist today. A reconstruction of the Anglo-Saxon village has been created on the site and gives a good impression of the way buildings were grouped and how people might have lived.

POWER AND POLITICS

As already mentioned, many early settlement patterns were influenced by the need for defence. This defence was not always primarily for the security of the population as a whole, but rather for the maintenance of power in the hands of a few members of the ruling minority; for example, feudal lords. Therefore the relationships between buildings could both increase security from threats from outside and also establish and maintain power structures within the settlement.

As the levels of instability and conflict in an area diminished, the defences are often retained or even created as symbolic statements of power, identity and independence. The internal 'defences' often remain in subtle and significant ways, for example walls and gates to the homes of important people, and grand boulevards and triumphal arches, as statements of national and civic power and pride, such as the Arc de Triomphe and the Champs-Elysées in Paris.

As countries developed more structured systems of government and institutions of the state, these found expression in a variety of forms, all confirming their importance and status. Even places of learning, schools, libraries and museums were created in ways which established their place and importance in the hierarchy of public buildings. Often investment in public or civic areas and buildings can be seen to assume great symbolic significance, not only establishing the position of the town or city concerned, but also as a monument to those in power or political positions at the time. These forces can be seen throughout history from earliest times and can still be observed today. The competing political ideologies of capitalism and communism have also influenced the shapes of settlements, ranging from planned towns and public housing to corporate headquarters, private suburbs and business parks.

SPIRITUAL INFLUENCES AND RELIGIOUS POWER

Many of our oldest archaeological remains are a testament to the power of the spiritual and religious beliefs of the human race. These beliefs exert strong influences upon the shapes of settlements and the arrangement of buildings and spaces between them. Many places were originally conceived for religious, ceremonial or processional use, and they helped to establish and maintain hierarchical and social structures. The positions of temples, mosques, monasteries and cathedrals and the arrangements of associated spaces and buildings around them were carefully planned to provide the physical space and relationships for ceremonial use and also to convey symbolic meaning and show the power of the church. These religious precincts were often of distinctly different layout and form from the humble buildings which clustered around them.

The influence of religion extended throughout the surrounding community in both the physical presence of church, shrines or statues and the 'administration' or urban divisions into parishes, guzar or mohalla.

As Kostoff put it: 'The power of religion to organize the urban populace at the neighbourhood level is a staple of the pre-industrial city.'[3]

CASE STUDY – MEDINA, MALTA

Medina is the oldest city in Malta, and may have been established during the Bronze Age. It was definitely inhabited in Punic and Roman times. It is a fortified city occupying a hilltop location with high defensive walls and deep defensive ditches. The first walls were built by the

Arab inhabitants of Malta and these walls were strengthened by Norman occupiers. Two gates give controlled access to the city, which is sometimes known as the 'Silent City' because of its air of mystery and the reverence which its streets inspire. The main space, St Paul's Square, provides a wonderful piazza from which a variety of narrow streets and alleys link to the gates and walls, whence extensive views of the surrounding countryside can be gained. The narrow streets give shade and induce air movement providing a natural 'air-conditioning'.

The form of the cathedral combined with the hilltop location of the city creates a powerful image which can be seen for several miles.

Figure 4.1 Medina, Malta: a long-distance view. (David Chapman.)

As a place to study, Medina demonstrates a multitude of the characteristics of historic settlements world-wide. It shows:

- defensive location;
- layering of periods of development;
- modifying environmental comfort and conditions;
- strong townscape character;
- imageability.

The economic well-being and vitality of settlements is an essential requirement for their long-term success and robustness. At some times and in some places this economic expansion drives the development patterns of settlements. This can be readily seen in the thousands of terraced houses and the few remaining back-to-back houses, spawned by the industrial revolution and the need to house a multitude of workers

COMMERCIAL DEVELOPMENT, PROFIT AND LOSS

close to the new factories. World-wide there are many swiftly expanding cities whose populations are being housed in rapidly developed planned areas or haphazard shanty towns.

Development has increasingly become a business activity in its own right and the economics of development in a market economy usually dictates whether development takes place, where it takes place and its form and specification. Clearly market pressures and demand strongly influence this but the connection is imperfect. Often national and international financial regimes, taxation systems and schemes of grant aid exert influential pressures on individual and corporate decision-making. In some cases developers have overestimated the growth in demand, for example with the massive oversupply of office space in London, especially the Canary Wharf development in Docklands. In other cases developers can be 'market makers', for example in urban regeneration schemes where land assembly, development strategies and a vision can stimulate economic activity in an area of decline.

PHILOSOPHIES AND BELIEFS

The patterns of settlement and development have been influenced in many subtle ways by the philosophical beliefs of people and communities, and in turn they have helped shape these beliefs. It has been claimed that the process of urbanization has made city dwellers feel differently from country dwellers: 'The City is possessed of a unique culture, Urbanism is free intellect. It is participating democracy.'[4]

There are also many examples of philosophical beliefs being held in principle about the development of settlements themselves and the societies which they support. These Utopian beliefs have sometimes remained as dreams but others have been realized to different extents and with varying success. Examples include the philanthropically inspired settlements of the industrial revolution and the Garden City movement, such as Port Sunlight and Letchworth, respectively.

LAYERING OF BUILT ENVIRONMENTS
EARLY SETTLEMENT PATTERNS

Many societies originated (and some continue) as nomadic people moving from one temporary settlement to another. As agricultural skills and animal husbandry improved there was a growing advantage in staying in a fixed location. Early settlements and buildings in these societies tended to employ building materials and techniques derived from earlier nomadic times. Timber and straw post houses were used by Anglo-Saxons, for example at West Stowe in Suffolk. Other societies, notably the Romans, developed much more substantial building techniques using stone and mortar to produce permanent structures. Nevertheless, settlements of any period can decline and become abandoned, for instance as a result of plague, natural disaster or exhaustion of the soil or a local mineral.

Archaeological evidence of the various layers of settlement and development which have been overlain one upon another, over many centuries, is often fragmentary. It is of great importance for anyone concerned with the study of, or proposals for, the built environment to try to understand the underlying factors and the influences of each period of development, and to look for the lessons which might be learned. Many of the features of the past have been lost or buried beneath later developments but many also exert powerful influences upon the development pattern and the character and appearance of places today.

Cromford, a small village, developed in the late eighteenth and early nineteenth centuries, as a very early industrial village around water-powered cotton spinning mills.

It makes a fascinating study for the way in which the location was utilized to provide the site for the new mills, to draw power from a small stream and to provide workers' housing, market place, parish church and mill owner's 'castle' in subtly planned relationships.

CASE STUDY – CROMFORD, DERBYSHIRE

WORKPIECE 4.2

STUDYING A SMALL SETTLEMENT

Select a small settlement or a distinct part of a settlement which you will be able to study conveniently. Consider and list the following factors:

● What factors led to settlement having occured in that place?
- Why was the place chosen?
- What were its advantages and disadvantages?

● What influenced the pattern of development?
- What climatic influences were there?
- Who were the main decision makers at each stage of development?
- Are there key factors which affected development physically or philosophically?
- Are there any distinctively different patterns of development in the area?

The location of settlements within the landscape related to lines of communication whether on foot or by some form of assistance.

Indeed, strategic positions at crossroads or river fords often became locations for settlements and the exchange of information and trade. As modes of transport developed, so did the nature of the links. Roads developed in number and width, canals were created and railways established. These involved massive investment and though many are

COMMUNICATION AND INFRASTRUCTURE

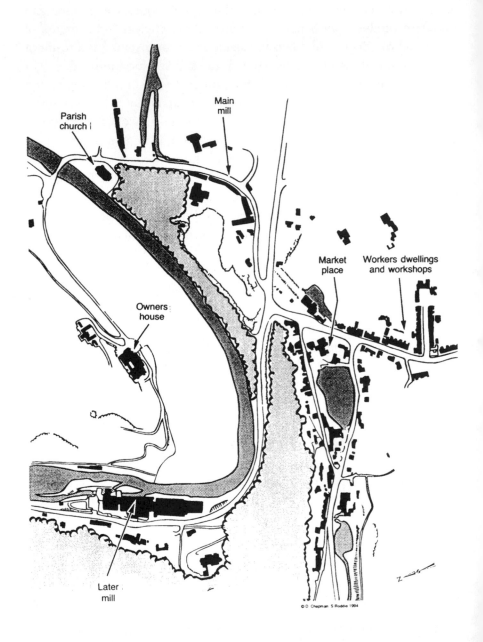

Figure 4.2 Plan of Cromford, Derbyshire. (Steve Roddie.)

still in active use, some have become redundant or underused. Nevertheless their physical form continues to exert a strong influence upon the shape and location of development today.

Figure 4.3   View of Cromford, Derbyshire. (David Chapman.)

Below many of our 'modern' cities, quite ancient systems of drainage and sewerage can be found, side by side with the latest fibre optic technology. These systems of infrastructure provide access, deliver power and information and take away unwanted material. The location of settlements responded to opportunities within the landform and technological capabilities of the time. The systems of infrastructure which now exist will exert considerable influence upon the development patterns of the future as well as in some cases causing major problems regarding maintenance and upgrading.

The fortunes of societies and their settlements are rarely stable for long periods: they wax and wane. There is a general growth in population world-wide but some places have experienced significant decline in population and economic activity. Growth creates its own problems and so does decline. Anyone interested in the processes of urban change seeks to understand the characteristics of growth and decline. The 'ghost town' of North America can be compared with the dereliction of some inner city areas in Britain. These declining areas deserve careful consideration and management. They may present a range of possibilities which can be teased out, for example the creation of urban wildlife areas, new open spaces or recreation facilities.

GROWTH AND DECLINE

Where decline occurs in a dense urban townscape, this can have a profound effect upon the character and quality of the place. The historic cores of towns can decline and buildings become abandonded or demolished. The effect of this upon distinctive urban forms creates issues for public policy and for architectural design.

BUILDINGS AND SPACE

In *The City Assembled*, Spiro Kostoff describes the various elements of urban form including the edges of settlements, the public places and the streets.[3] One of the most significant characteristics of each of these elements is the space between the buildings – the spaces enclosed by the buildings in the landscape within which the buildings are located. Through successive periods of development quite distinctive approaches have been adopted to the relationship between buildings and space. Industrial buildings or small groups of buildings have been arranged to create secure, enclosed and sheltered spaces (for example, a traditional group of farm buildings) and whole towns and cities have been arranged with these objectives in mind (for example, Medina in Malta). These tried and tested approaches to urban space were thrown over in the early part of the twentieth century by 'modernists' who adopted quite a different approach to the form of buildings and the spaces between them. Essentially buildings were increased in height to release space at ground level for open space. This resulted in tall buildings being placed in a 'landscaped' setting and the creation of few, if any, enclosed streets or public places. These large landscaped spaces tended to lack the definition, ownership and vitality of the traditional urban form of streets and public places.

WORKPIECE 4.3

EXAMINING DIFFERENT SETTLEMENT OR DEVELOPMENT PATTERNS.

Find two areas which show contrasting patterns of development. These may have been identified from Workpiece 4.2 but you may prefer to look further afield.

List the main characteristics of each area.
Describe the main difference between the areas.
Consider the reasons for the differences.

THE QUALITIES OF PLACES

The qualities of places as we experience them today are influenced by the layers of development that have lead to their current state. Understanding the processes that have occurred helps us to interpret what has happened in the past and also to define questions of the present and future. Each society and individual has immediate and personal needs from places and it is the way in which settlements satisfy these needs today which is immediately important.

The public streets and spaces of settlements can be the meeting ground for members of local communities and for visitors. Some places are more frequently used by local people and others receive a higher proportion of strangers. As Jane Jacobs said, 'One of the chief requirements is to keep the city safe for strangers,' [5] but we are also concerned about the safety and sense of security of local people of all ages.

    The processes of settlement and development often define 'territory' or ownership. The physical form and relationships between public, semi-public and private space can create a sense or lack of 'defensible space' and thus the feeling of insecurity or vulnerability.[6] In recent residential developments it has been suggested that this concept could be extended to incorporate measures to 'design against crime'.

The physical form and structure of places is only one component of the character and quality of that place. Kostoff reminds us of Botero's insistence that 'the message of the city is in its human activity, in processes, military, recreational and economic'.[3]

    At times of growth and prosperity, the vitality of the human activities is an inextricable component of the quality of places. At other times the vitality of a place may decline. The reasons for this may vary and may be short or long term in nature. Nevertheless settlements have a tendency to continue and to renew themselves either by chance or by deliberate intervention. In the most established settlements it is noticeable that their robustness and ability to weather periods of decline is often connected with the diversity of the activities upon which they depend.

The locations of settlements were frequently selected for the environmental benefits they offered. The relationships between buildings and spaces modify the microclimate of the place and can improve or diminish environmental comfort. Buildings can provide shelter or produce air turbulence. They can enclose suntraps or create shade. The ability to influence air temperatures and air movement can have significant benefits for environmental comfort in a variety of situations including temperate areas, hot dry areas and hot humid areas. Each climate requires an individual approach to creating the microclimate locally.

SENSORY QUALITIES

The pleasures of the warming sun or a cooling breeze add to the sensory enjoyment of a place. All of our senses contribute to our understanding and reaction to a place. The aromatic qualities, both pleasant and unpleasant, influence our perceptions as do the textures of surfaces and materials which we both see and feel. The sense of hearing responds to the activities going on and the sounds they generate, ranging from traffic noise to the sound of falling water in a fountain. The taste of salt water on the air and the feeling of a cool breeze against the face contrast deeply with the inhalation of diesel fumes in a busy street, but each sensation adds to our appreciation of the qualities of a place.

VISUAL DELIGHT

Much of the theoretical and critical evaluation of architecture and urban space has been concerned with visual characteristics. These are perhaps the most obvious and 'controllable' ingredients of places but, as has been shown, they are perhaps only the visible tip of a very large 'iceberg' which contains many other factors.

The visual appearance can seem to be almost accidental, as in organically developed settlements, or deliberately created as in planned towns. The principal visual characteristics of places are created by the different views experienced by people in the area. Types of view can be more subtly described as glimpses, open views, vistas, panoramas etc.

The way in which our view of a place is framed or open is one component of the experience. The other is the context of the 'view'. This context may be plain and simple or varied and complex, accidental or composed. All of the elements in view are important: the objects, the subdivisions of their form and mass, colours, textures and the constantly changing angle of vision for different viewers and the changing effects of light and darkness.

UNDERSTANDING PLACES

PERCEPTION OF URBAN FORMS

There are various ways in which it has been suggested that we perceive and understand urban form. Perhaps one of the most simple and robust is Kevin Lynch's suggestion in *Image of the City*, that there are five key elements to that perception; landmarks, paths, edges, nodes and districts.[7] Basic though this concept is, it offers a way to appreciate places and provides a simple notation for analysis of existing places and design proposals.

The make-up of settlements can be analysed by examining the individual elements which make it up but we actually react to the overall image of the place. Lynch introduced the term **imageability** as shorthand for the way we perceive settlements and the characteristics which give us an image of a place, either positive or negative.[7]

SURVEY: EXPLORING THE ELEMENTS OF URBAN FORM AND IMAGE

Take the small settlement which you selected in Workpiece 4.2 and carry out a survey based upon Kevin Lynch's five key elements of urban form. Using a 1:2500 scale plan, mark up the key nodes, path, edges, landmarks and districts.

Then write a brief description of the main characteristics of the area which contribute towards its image and sense of place.

TOWNSCAPE

The combination of building form, the spaces between buildings and the elements contained within them was termed **townscape** by Gordon Cullen.[8] He emphasized the ingredients which help to make enjoyable and 'successful' townscapes and examined the ways in which we experience them. In doing this he identified three components:

- the sense of place;
- the content of the place;
- serial vision.

URBAN SPACE

In 1748 Giambattista Nolli produced a plan of Rome which showed in 'figure ground' the relationship between open space (both external and internal) and private internal space within buildings. This plan demonstrates graphically how important it is to understand the form of the spaces between buildings as well as the form of buildings themselves. The shape of the spaces in three dimensions creates a variety of spatial experiences (as Cullen said: 'a journey through pressures and vacuums'). This urban space is in fact one of the main contributors to our perception of places. Although in declining areas the townscape and urban space may be eroded, it is probable that in vibrant and vigorous places the urban space will make a positive contribution to that vitality, either as a result of successive periods of change and improvement or as part of a planned composition. Rob Krier has examined the form of urban space in some detail, principally in terms of its spatial characteristics and the way buildings modify or inform our perception of that space.[9] Cullen and Lynch,[7,8] would of course remind us that the content of the space and its accessibility and 'legibility' are of equal importance.

85

RESPONSIVE ENVIRONMENTS

The physical form of settlements, the contents of the place and the way people use it has been described by Bentley *et al.* as the 'responsiveness of the environment'.[1] They have suggested that, to be truly responsive, places should possess certain characteristics which can be briefly described as follows:

- Legibility
- Permeability
- Variety
- Robustness
- Richness
- Visual appropriateness
- Personalization.

These simple concepts are easy to use in the appraisal of existing settlements and provide an excellent guide for anyone altering an existing development or creating a new one.

CASE STUDY – CUMBERNAULD NEW TOWN

New towns have been created at various times and in many places throughout the world. In the UK after the second world war there was a significant period of New Town building to rehouse people displaced by war damage and slum clearance in the older industrial cities. These towns were conceived as self-sufficient units of limited size and were planned as totally new entities. They embodied many of the concepts which had been advanced by the Utopians and modernists, in particular the attention paid to providing for the motor vehicle. This involved pedestrian and vehicle segregation and a highly accessible system of road hierarchies. Residential neighbourhoods were sized to be able to support a local centre, school and the like. 'Zones' for industrial and recreational uses were integrated into the plans, which tended to create low-density dispersed settlement patterns. Milton Keynes, one of the later examples, is particularly notable in the latter sense.

Cumbernauld New Town was designated in 1956 and was intended to house 50 000 and subsequently 70 000 inhabitants, in Central Scotland. The chosen site was an exposed hilltop, which is somewhat surprising considering the extreme local weather conditions. This new town was planned at relatively high densities compared with the others and has a quite compact form. The road hierarchy is almost entirely separated from the pedestrian. In the central area the main level for pedestrians is above the vehicles and in residential areas separation is

Figure 4.4 View of Cumbernauld Town Centre, a Scottish new town. (Tom Muir.)

obtained by bridges and subways. Marked improvement in road safety must be set against reduced personal security and environmental quality. Residential areas were influenced by the work of Clarence Stein in America: houses face on to footpaths, with car access in rear courts. The town centre was planned to house all of the shops and public buildings under one roof and comprised two parallel buildings either side of an 'urban motorway'. All vehicles and servicing are kept at ground level and people move around on decks, stairs, escalators and lifts at upper levels with bridge links between the buildings.

The creation of a new town is an enormous enterprise involving huge investments of human, financial and material capital. The scale of change provides the opportunity to adopt new approaches to long-standing problems. There is also the risk that unintentionally the nature or social effects of our decisions could be misjudged. One of the great lessons of the late twentieth century may be the recognition of the possible danger that large-scale changes in complete historic settlements, or the attempt to create major new settlements, may cause unsatisfactory physical and social conditions and that it is better to 'avoid the trauma of too great a change at any one time'.[10]

HOW ARE THESE PROCESSES OF CHANGE SHAPED TODAY?

In Chapter 5 we shall explore development processes and planning systems. These processes are shaped by a variety of 'actors' and in many countries there is a democratic framework of legislation and controls which shape these processes. Planning systems are concerned with a range of issues, from broad strategic policies to potentially detailed 'development controls'.

Development controls can clearly affect the future locations and patterns of development and the detailed characterisitics of that development, as well as regulating the processes of change in long-established places.

SUMMARY

The physical place which we inhabit affects the quality of our lives, our health and our freedom. There are many influences and forces at work to shape the pattern of human settlement and the form of public spaces and relationships between buildings. The influence of natural forces is enormous and human interventions are strongly constrained by it. Nevertheless the social, spiritual, cultural and economic aspirations of different societies exert great influences upon the shape of built environments within the natural environment. Developments have grown and been adapted over time and layers of new development often lie over the old. The resultant places may possess enjoyable or unenjoyable characteristics and in order to understand them it is important to explore why and how they developed, what their good and bad qualities are, and how we might influence future changes to achieve enjoyable places.

Through the chapter we have:

- identified the forces in the natural environment which affect the pattern and form of settlement;
- considered the effects of human aspirations and intervention upon the built environment;
- examined the characteristics of 'good' people-friendly places;
- explored some of the qualities of places and how they may influence future plans, decisions and designs.

KEY CONCEPTS

- **Many forces interact to shape the natural and the built environment.**
- **The influences of nature are profound and unique to each part of the world.**
- **The relationships between people and their spiritual, philosophical and personal beliefs or motives contribute to a**

continuous process of decision-making and change in our built environments.

● Settlements evolve and develop, creating complex layers and patterns of activity and development, the future patterns inevitably being influenced by the past.

● People need basic safety and comfort from the environment before they can enjoy its aesthetic and sensory qualities.

● Understanding the quality places can have, both good and bad, is an essential ability for anyone involved with shaping built environments.

● The environments we inhabit and enjoy result from a complex interaction of many variables. We cannot understand, influence or control all of the factors involved.

● Everyone involved with our built environment has a role to play. We can all shape the processes of change and contribute to the vitality of places. Understanding the qualities, complexities and our potential contribution to the future of our settlements is valuable for us all.

REFERENCES

1.   Bentley, I., Alcock, I., Murrain, P., McGlynn, S. and Smith, G. (1991) *Responsive Environments – a manual for designers*, Architectural Press, London.
2.   Whitehand, J.W.R (1991) *The Making of the Urban Landscape*, Blackwell.
3.   Kostoff, S. (1922) *The City Assembled*, Thames and Hudson.
4.   Spengler, O. (1970) *Urban man and society*, Alfred A. Knope.
5.   Jacobs, J. (1961) *The Death and Life of Great American Cities*, Penguin.
6.   Newman, O. (1972) *Defensible Space: People and Design in the Violent City*, Architectural Press, London.
7.   Lynch, K. (1960) *The Image of the City*, M.I.T/Harvard University Press, Mass.
8.   Cullen, G. (1971) *The Concise Townscape*, Architectural Press, London.
9.   Krier, R. (1979) *Urban Space*, Academy Editions, London.
10. Tibbalds, F. (1992) *Making People-friendly Towns*, Longman.

FURTHER READING

Burke, G. (1971) *Towns in the Making*, Edward Arnold.
Chapman, D.W and Larkham, P. (1994) *Understanding Urban Design*, School of Planning, University of Central England, Birmingham.
Owen, S. (1991) *Planning Settlements Naturally*, Packard.

5

UK DEVELOPMENT PROCESSES IN AN INTERNATIONAL CONTEXT

JEAN BADMAN

THEME

The UK has developed a particular approach to managing and controlling the development process. Whatever our role in the environment, it is essential to understand the nature of this process and the ideas and legislation behind it. How does this compare with the process in other countries? This chapter provides a basic account of the development process in the UK and highlights some of the key similarities in a number of other countries.

OBJECTIVES

After reading this chapter you should be able to:

● understand the nature of development processes in the UK;

● understand the roles of professionals within this and in particular the nature of government legislation affecting it;

● understand the basis of UK planning law including development control;

● identify key similarities and differences between UK practice and those in other countries;

● appreciate the need for and nature of EU legislation, and the implication of this for the future.

The development of the landscape and townscape has evolved over the centuries, beginning with human attempts to utilize natural features of the earth's environment to provide shelter, e.g. caves, mud huts and tree houses. As technology has developed and expectations have changed, so the nature of development has often become increasingly more complex and sophisticated.

Structures were created and land developed initially to sustain life, the provision of shelter and food being of the highest importance. However, as trading became established so settlements started to have economic significance, with villages and towns located at the meeting of routeways growing into thriving markets. With technological advances and the expansion of commmunications the development of large towns and cities has become a feature of modern civilisation throughout the world. The nature and timing of such development, however, has varied greatly across the face of the globe affected by a wide range of factors including the location and scale of the area, topographical and climatic conditions and religious ideologies.

The state of California, for example, owes much of its initial development to the gold rush of the nineteenth century with thousands of prospectors spending new-found wealth on various land and property developments. A more recent example in the UK is the dramatic influence that the discovery of oil in the North Sea has had on the city of Aberdeen, where vast commercial, industrial and residential schemes have been the result of a buoyant local economy. Political attitudes have been increasingly important in recent years with differing policies towards social, economic and environmental issues influencing the establishment of towns.

WORKPIECE 5.1

A TOWN DEVELOPMENT

Using a town or city you know well, identify the factors that have influenced its development to date.

From memory, draw a plan of the town highlighting the main features and indicate the main constraint that you feel will influence any future management.

POTENTIAL FOR INVESTMENT

A feature of western development activity over the twentieth century has been its potential for investment. In Britain individual homes have been seen as a person's largest investment for the future with good security and opportunities for growth. However, the experience of the late 1980s, with many houses falling in relative value, has placed a question mark against this. Larger scale developments involving commercial office blocks or shopping centres, leisure or industrial schemes often attract the interest of the major insurance companies or pension funds who see property as an important component of their investment portfolio.

As development has increased in scale and complexity, so it has become more important to ensure that the quality of the environment can be maintained and enhanced, that buildings perform in an efficient manner and that the health and safety of individual users and the community at large can be maintained.

Across the world there are numerous rules and regulations in place which attempt to control land use and development. Some are very sophisticated and operate through government whilst others are more ad hoc with individual landowners controlling the nature of activities.

In Britain the system of development control and planning has evolved from what was essentially private control, e.g. that operated by the Church, the monarchy and individual landowners. Concern for public health and poor housing conditions in the nineteenth century resulted in changes in urban design. Planning the environment as a whole was anticipated to influence the behaviour of society and the public control of resource allocation was to be fundamental to achieving a balanced approach. The current system of public control is operated by government at various levels.[1] Any private controls that do exist, including restrictions on lease terms, restrictive covenants or easements, operate within the framework of public control.

DEVELOPMENT AND CONTROL THROUGH THE AGES

Early control over the development of land and buildings was the responsibility of landowners but even as far back as 450 BC Hippodamus of Miletus was embarking on a form of planning of towns which was to be influential in centuries to come. His plans for Piraeus, the port of Athens, used a grid pattern to provide an efficient use of land and allocated sites for public buildings.[2] Roman new towns adopted the same principles but their greater sophistication in engineering allowed quite large areas of towns to benefit from running water and a drainage system. There is still evidence today of the influence of the Romans in determining the twentieth century development of some of our towns. Cities like York and Colchester, Canterbury and St Albans have grown around typical Roman features including town walls, castles and theatres which have today become important tourist attractions and are often protected by statute.

The mediaeval period in Britain showed substantial town development with the expansion of many existing towns (known as adaptive or organic towns) and also new town development. Land ownership was still in the hands of the monarchy, the lords of the manor and the Church and such controls that did exist were in the main piecemeal and limited to specific areas. However, in the case of the new towns (planned or planted towns), e.g. Ludlow, Hull and Berwick-on-Tweed, considerable effort was put into deciding on building density, building lines, land use, access, water provision and appropriate fortifications resulting in a more symmetrical if perhaps less interesting development.

Adaptive towns, by contrast, were far less predictable with winding streets and overhanging buildings leading out on to large, open market squares. The wealthy families and some religious communities might occupy properties in large grounds on the outskirts of towns but more central areas often had properties which packed into narrow streets with only small passages allowing access to rear gardens. A street scene of contrast and continuity is therefore typical of most adaptive mediaeval towns. In towns such as Warwick and Leominster, for example, the church might dominate the market square, which would be located at the junction of a number of streets where buildings would be packed tightly together to give a sense of continuity (as well as keeping the elements at bay).[2] Mediaeval towns, however, were clearly lacking in any real provision of public services or control, with the result that street paving was a rarity, streets were hardly ever drained or cleaned and piped water was not a feature of most towns. The resulting environment was dirty, smelly and often a health hazard, as well as a fire hazard.

The Renaissance period of town development introduced an increasing scale to towns and cities with wider streets, taller buildings, and symmetrical building facades. This was in part a response to the increasing growth in non-pedestrian traffic. In addition it was during this period that many formal gardens were constructed as settings for palaces or country houses. Today palaces like the Tuileries in Paris, the Palace of Versailles, Hampton Court, Chatsworth and Longleat remain favourite attractions for tourists and represent the best work of the landscape gardeners of the period.[2]

In 1580 Queen Elizabeth I of England made a proclamation that was subsequently incorporated into an Act of Parliament that attempted to stop any new building within 3 miles of the gates of London. Whilst not particularly successful, it could perhaps be likened to one of the aims of twentieth century Green Belt policy in England and Wales, which is to restrict the growth of cities. The proclamation also established the principle that all families should have a home of their own and not be forced to live in multi-household tenement blocks. This can perhaps be seen as one of the earliest attempts to introduce formal control to land, even though it applied only to London.

The Classical Period is renowned for its town improvement schemes throughout the country including Bath, Edinburgh, Bristol, Cheltenham, Droitwich and Leamington. During the last few decades of the eighteenth century and early part of the nineteenth century, property development became a prominent feature of many towns and cities. Land was acquired on 99-year building leases and developments such as Queen Square in Bristol, Royal Crescent in Bath and Portland Place in London were undertaken. Speculative developers like Thomas Cubitt organized building work in a particularly sophisticated manner for the nineteenth century, maintaining a permanent staff of skilled tradesmen who could then be called upon to undertake any work as necessary. London squares such as Belgrave and Eaton are permanent reminders of Cubitt's work. Speculative development was quite carefully controlled during this period as most of the schemes were for the more affluent and influential members of society.

As the Industrial Revolution started to take hold, so it was accompanied by increases in population and a gradual shift of this population from rural to urban areas. This created the need for more living accommodation in towns but not in most cases adequate provision. Few employers saw it as their responsibility (Cadbury and Rowntree were very much in the minority) and neither did town councils. This left the opportunity for speculative developers to fill the gap. New developments were allowed to go ahead without any real controls and in consequence standards of building, sanitation, drainage and density were almost totally inadequate to cope with the needs of the growing population. The back-to-back houses of Britain's industrial towns were to become slums within a matter of decades. Various government commissions looked into the state of towns in terms of health and housing during the early part of the nineteenth century and gradually government legislation was introduced to promote municipal self-help and encourage better standards of living. These statutes of the nineteenth century were to be the beginnings of formal control by government over land and property, providing the basis from which modern planning legislation has evolved. In addition, the role of individuals such as Lord Shaftesbury, Octavia Hill, Edwin Chadwick and Robert Owen in influencing subsequent development should not be underestimated.

Speculative housing developments adopted 'tunnel back' houses as a response to by-laws introduced by local authorities. This is a term used to describe the kind of housing devised in the late nineteenth century by speculative builders to meet by-law standards with minimum expenditure. Acres and acres of this type of development led to a very monotonous landscape throughout many cities.[2] The introduction of gas and electricity, whilst providing tremendous benefits to residential and industrial activities, resulted in major problems of environmental pollution. Large areas of open space were lost in most cities but many public buildings were also constructed during this period as civic pride became an important issue and municipal authorities became more ambitious. Many of the most prestigious buildings in some towns originate from the nineteenth century including town halls and art galleries, museums, hotels and clubs, exhibition halls, hospitals and prisons, fire stations and law courts, and London in particular has especially fine examples of such public buildings including St Bartholomew's hospital, the Law Courts, the National Gallery, St Pancras station hotel and Crystal Palace. Birmingham was to become prominent during the Victorian period for its city improvement and redevelopment encouraged by Joseph Chamberlain: Corporation Street was developed as an important commercial area and still retains that importance today.

During the early part of the twentieth century most development was undertaken by private developers with only limited residential schemes for the working class being undertaken by public authorities. Laissez-faire urban growth was gradually being curtailed by the introduction of town planning legislation. Throughout the twentieth century the control of land use and building has become more sophisticated as developments have become increasingly complex and expensive to construct, with the potential financial gains and losses becoming substantial. The value of the Euston Centre, a large multi-storey office block in London, constructed in the 1960s was worth more than the largest UK company at that time – British Leyland.

Development is seen by many as a tremendous opportunity to make money, as witnessed by the growth in the number of property companies world-wide. Not all developments, however, make money or are even intended to make money. Many public developments have served a particular social purpose such as providing a community centre or prison, library or health centre, hospital or public park; others are essential to provide links with or services for existing developments such as power stations, water treatment works, airports and road and rail networks. Changing government policy in Britain towards privatizing some of these activities has added a new competitive edge to areas that have been controlled and subsidized by government for decades.

DEVELOPMENT – WHAT IS IT?

Development involves change to the physical environment, whether built or natural. It is concerned with the use of scarce resources which include raw materials, energy sources, money, people and of course land.

The *Oxford Dictionary* states that to develop means 'to build on or make fuller use of (land)' and that a development is 'an area of developed land'. Clearly these are rather broad definitions and do not reflect the complex nature of the process of development. The trend for public control over development has resulted in legislation providing an official definition of the term 'development'.

WORKPIECE 5.2

LEGISLATION

Which is the most recent piece of legislation to define the term development?
    What is the definition of development offered by the Act?
    Identify five different activities which in your opinion constitute development.

The development process involves a wide variety of players across the spectrum of the built environment and goes far beyond into the financial and legal professions. It involves both professionals and lay people not only playing a part within the process but also showing concern for the outcomes.

In recent years the term 'development' has tended to be associated with 'profit' and many people have been sceptical of the large-scale schemes that make substantial gains for the developers whilst at the same time having not altogether desirable environmental, social and economic consequences for the local community.

Development, however, is not always some parasitic activity which is only associated with speculation and profit and over the years there have been numerous examples of developments that have made a major contribution to the urban environment. Two of the most significant comprehensive town developments to occur in Britain during the eighteenth century were Bath (including the Royal Crescent) and Edinburgh (including Princes Street). In London, James Adams' Portland Place, part of the Marylebone Park estate, provided an imposing residential development just outside Regents Park and John Nash's Regent Street was to become significant both as a retail area and as a route for traffic.

Figure 5.1 A Nash terrace in London. (Peter Maddern.)

Figure 5.2 Bourneville, England – model village developed by industrialist George Cadbury. (Tom Muir.)

Industrialists like George Cadbury and William Lever developed model villages at Bournville in Birmingham and Port Sunlight just outside Manchester which proved inspirational to others, like Joseph Rowntree at New Earswick near York, to provide improved living conditions for their employees.

Unfortunately, we are more likely to remember the less attractive speculative developments of the nineteenth century which were to become the slums of the twentieth century, for example the Gorbals in Glasgow and Temple Street in Dublin where tenement buildings were soon to deteriorate resulting in many health related problems.

WHY DOES DEVELOPMENT OCCUR?

Essentially, development occurs due to the needs and demands of society or the speculation of the developer.

The development of shanty towns in Rio de Janeiro reflects the needs of a growing population who are caught in the poverty trap, with government doing little to help the housing problem. In Britain housing developments by the major residential developers reflect the socio-economic groupings of communities to allow a degree of choice in owner-occupation. Commercial property speculation, whilst offering the potential for huge gains, can result in developers being unable to dispose of or even complete developments. Some developers have gone into receivership through adopting what could be perhaps seen as a somewhat overzealous approach. The lack of any real strategic planning by some authorities can result in an oversupply of 'space'. The Canary Wharf project in London's Docklands, which was started during the 1980s, should have been a major success story for developers Olympia and York but problems with finance, delays in public infrastructure and the inability to let and/or sell large parts of the scheme proved catastrophic.

Normally most development occurs because of the potential for added value to be obtained from the process but the risks are still high and often factors which are outside the control of developers can spell disaster. Changes in interest rates, increases in oil prices, fluctuations in building costs or delays in completion are all factors which can turn profit into loss. The six-day war of 1973, which saw oil prices virtually double, resulted in the demise of hundreds of property companies. Some developments that are not necessarily built for profit, however, will provide an important service to the community and of course other profit-making activities. For example, public open space, community centres, libraries, museums and prisons are all essential to the efficient operation

Figure 5.3 Canary Wharf, London. (Tom Muir.)

of urban and rural environments. Infrastructure is essential as part of new development and in order to promote it. London Docklands is a prime example of how good infrastructure is essential to enable development and to provide a catalyst for it.

Development therefore contributes to the community through improved provision of buildings and infrastructure, through economic activity and the tax base and via employment. In recent years development has been largely funded through insurance companies and pension funds and this provides a further link with the community.

Recently there has been an increasing move to reflect environmental considerations in development proposals and this has been shown via the use of recycled materials in construction, changes in design, use of alternative energy sources and increasing legislative control.

So, what is the process necessary for development to occur? Who are the players in this process and what are their roles? What type of development will occur and where? How is this development controlled and monitored? This chapter attempts to answer these questions.

Development as an activity follows a series of stages, many of which run concurrently rather than in sequence. As such it is clear that the number of variables is high and hence the final output is the result of a series of complex and often interrelated decisions.

DEVELOPMENT PROCESS

INITIATIVE FOR DEVELOPMENT

The initiative for development may come from a number of sources: the would-be user, a third party who may be speculating on the demand for a particular land use (developer or agent), the owner of the land or a third party anticipating an improved value from a new use (again developers or agents, or the local authority may be involved).

One view of development suggests that it is dictated by planners, designed by architects and controlled financially by developers (often via their financiers). Is this really true?

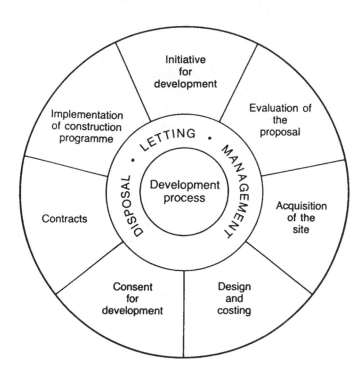

Figure 5.4   The development process.

STAGES IN THE DEVELOPMENT PROCESS

There are various stages in the process of development and at each stage there may be a number of 'players' involved. Aims and objectives frequently differ for each of the players and the final project is the result of reconciling these, although not always to the mutual satisfaction of all the parties.

The stages in the development process were indicated by Cadman and Austin-Crowe [3], and can be summarized as follows.

THE INITIATIVE FOR DEVELOPMENT   From whom? Landowner, occupier, local authority, developer, agent, other.

EVALUATION OF DEVELOPMENT POTENTIAL   Physical assessment of the site, legal assessment, financial assessment of the proposal.

SITE ACQUISITION   How? Can all the rights to the site be acquired? Will compulsory purchase be necessary? Can the necessary finance be raised? Is there support for the scheme?

DESIGNING AND COSTING THE SCHEME   These become progressively more detailed as the development proposal increases in certainty. Design/development briefs may be produced.

OBTAINING CONSENT TO DEVELOP   Need for planning approval, what is involved? Other consents, e.g. building regulations, fire regulations, health and safety regulations, Listed Building or other conservation consent.

SIGNING OF VARIOUS INTERRELATED CONTRACTS   Finance, site acquisition, materials, subcontracts, legal.

IMPLEMENTATION OF THE CONSTRUCTION PROGRAMME   Coordination and management are particularly important aspects of any project, ensuring that there is an ability to respond to factors of change that may affect the success of the scheme. Luck is another aspect: the long time period frequently associated with many projects often results in the unpredictable occurring, sometimes to the benefit of the project but more often to its detriment.

DISPOSAL/LETTING/MANAGEMENT   This is not an end phase but should be considered fully at a project's inception. It is extremely difficult to speculate on the long-term success of many projects, with years often elapsing before a scheme is fully let or sold.

There are various players involved in the process of development and their aims and interests can vary substantially. A clear understanding of how these interests may interact and the potential conflicts that may occur should allow us to respond more effectively to problems.[5]

THE PLAYERS

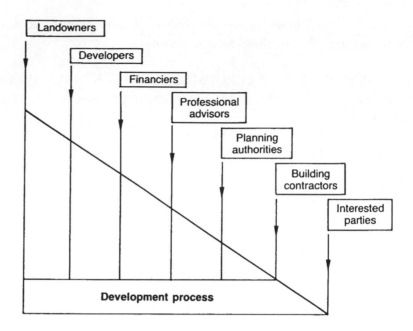

Figure 5.5   Players in the development process.

LANDOWNERS   Landowners may be active in promoting development or alternatively may provide a significant obstacle to any proposal. Motivation can play a major role in any decision to develop. Financial interests are not always the highest priority for many landowners who are influenced by the desire to maintain family ties or traditions or who have strong environmental views. In cases where the proposed site for development is in multiple ownership, acquisition is frequently a rather long and often expensive business.

DEVELOPERS   No developer goes into a scheme expecting to make a loss and no one would wish to finance such a proposal. Hence all developers aim to make some profit, however small. Developers may, however, merely develop and then dispose of the development using the income to part-finance the next scheme. Housebuilders are good examples of this type of developer. Other developers, particularly as they grow in size, will retain some financial interest in certain schemes, thereby investing in any future success or failure. Some very large companies do little or no new building, concentrating on refurbishment and managing their portfolio. Some developers build for their own occupation, for example food retailers. Others may specialize in a particular type of development like retailing but have an increasing tendency to diversify into other areas, such as office schemes.

Some developers only operate in a very limited geographical area whilst others may operate worldwide. Developers may be private, public, quangos (quasi autonomous non-governmental organizations) or a form of partnership and can vary dramatically in size and function.

PLANNING AUTHORITIES Policies to promote economic well-being, social benefit and environmental enhancement are produced and evaluated over time and frequently generate development activity. However, there is often conflict between individual user requirements in terms of form, function and economy and the local planning authority, who is looking at the wider picture.

With limited exceptions all development activity requires prior approval from the local planning authority and the benefit of planning permission can greatly enhance the value of land. Permission for residential development on agricultural land has in the past resulted in as much as a 50-fold increase in land value. Development Plans are expected to play a much more significant role in determining planning permissions in future and hence the designation of land for a particular purpose in the Plan will affect its value as well as planning permission.

FINANCIERS Where does the money come from? Few developers can finance schemes without borrowing. Long-term and short-term finance come from various sources both within the UK and overseas, for example insurance companies, pension funds, merchant banks, building societies, government grants, EU funding and many more. Imaginative financial packages can often improve the potential for profit (or breakeven) but often lending institutions are reluctant to take risks if they have suffered huge losses in previous property speculations. Some lenders can be an important element of a development partnership.

BUILDING CONTRACTORS There are various specialist activities within the development process which will require clear contractual relationships between the parties. The ability to coordinate the activities efficiently, ensuring jobs are undertaken at the appropriate time, materials are available and payments are made when necessary, is a key role of the project manager. Penalties for failure to complete by the due date can be avoided and in some cases huge bonuses can be achieved through early completion. The developers who reconstructed the Santa Monica highway in California after the earthquake in 1993 finished over six months early – to a bonus of $12million.

PROFESSIONAL ADVISORS   Who are they? They are architects, building surveyors, estate managers, quantity surveyors, engineers, accountants, tax advisors, planning consultants etc. Do not forget the end user. Frequently the occupier is not given enough consideration but can play an invaluable role in helping to create an efficient, attractive and easily disposable asset.

INTERESTED PARTIES   Other parties may be interested in the scheme merely for the benefits it will bring but often they are apathetic and it is more likely that the interest will be less supportive. The potential delaying power of protestors can cost time and money and, whilst some objectors may be of only minimal concern, others such as major conservation groups (for example, the Victorian Society or the National Trust) carry considerable political weight.

It is abundantly clear that any successful development requires not only skill but that little bit of luck. Durability and flexibility should prove to be the key ingredients for attracting investors but no development is without risk.

One has to question:

● Who wins and who loses in the development process?
● Are there any benefits?
● What are the costs and who pays?
● What price do we pay for progress?

WORKPIECE 5.3

COST–BENEFIT ANALYSIS

The development of out-of-town food superstores has been a feature of the last 20 years and their possible impact on existing town centres has often been an issue for discussion.

Using a development you are familiar with, critically assess the costs and benefits of such a scheme.

NATURE OF CONTROLS (PRIVATE AND PUBLIC)

Why do controls over development exist? Controls over development have been introduced in Britain to ensure that adequate consideration is given to issues of public health, safety, performance, quality and environment. These controls are normally introduced by statute or statutory instrument and enforced where appropriate by local authorities. They include the following:

- Public Health Acts
- Planning Acts
- Building Regulations
- Fire Regulations
- Other controls.

The nature of these controls influences such things as land use, density of development, the interrelationship of buildings and areas within both the urban and rural scene, the type, form and function of buildings and the materials used for construction.

The result of these controls is, in the main, a built environment that can provide a high standard of living and working for a society with increasingly complex needs and expectations. The importance of the relationship between land use and transportation policies is increasingly being recognized but research is still needed to examine the most sustainable strategies to adopt in the future.

Safety controls will include means of escape, design and materials, and access. Quality controls will include noise pollution, daylight indicators, proximity to neighbours or adjoining uses, and nature of materials. Health controls will include drainage, sanitation, water and designs of buildings. Performance controls will include materials, design features, location and orientation of buildings. Environmental controls will include density and function of development and protection of land, buildings, flora and fauna.

The development industry, whether it be private or public, must reflect these controls in their schemes and whilst there will always be a cost of maintaining or improving standards the benefits should far outweigh any problems.

WORKPIECE 5.4

STATUTORY CONTROLS

Identify the current statutes and statutory instruments that control the use and development of land and property having regard to public health, safety, performance, quality and environment.

Discuss the view that conservation controls and fire regulations can often be in conflict, with the result that it will be economically unviable to develop some properties for alternative uses.

PLANNING AND DEVELOPMENT CONTROL IN ENGLAND AND WALES

Why have a system of public control over land and property? Private control over land has been in evidence for many hundreds of years but public control has predominantly been a feature of the twentieth century.

The statutory system of planning in the UK has existed broadly in its current form since 1947 and is based on the premise that all development will require the approval of appropriate planning authorities before it can take place. Planning authority decisions are taken in the context of Development Plans which are produced to give a long-term view of future needs in a particular area. Development Plans essentially operate at two levels: the strategic level, where the plan indicates broad policies for issues such as the economy or the environment, and the local level, where policies are more detailed and area specific concerned with housing or retail proposals for example. The Development Plan contains both written and diagrammatic representation of information and is used as the basis on which to determine planning applications.

Developers seeking planning approval for a site in England or Wales should have regard to the contents of the Development Plan as stated in Section 54A of the 1990 Town and Country Planning Act.

Obtaining local authority approval for a proposal requires developers to submit a planning application which will then normally be considered by the planning committee (this is made up of lay councillors, who are advised by professional planning officers). A decision should be received within 8 weeks of receipt of the application (80% are) but for major schemes the time can be considerably longer – 6–9 months in some cases. The Department of the Environment produces quarterly statistics to monitor the nature and number of planning applications in the system at any one time.

Developers may apply for outline planning permission, which is merely obtaining agreement in principle to a proposal (approvals will be accompanied by a series of reserved matters which will need subsequent consideration before development can proceed). Alternatively, full planning approval may be sought, but this requires a more detailed application and hence is more expensive initially. Some proposals where the development involves a change of use will always require a full application. The format for submission and the consideration of an application is shown in Figure 5.6.

Around 500 000 planning applications are dealt with by local authorities in England and Wales each year and of these over 83% are successful, although it is quite usual for certain conditions to be attached. Conditions might include access and parking requirements,

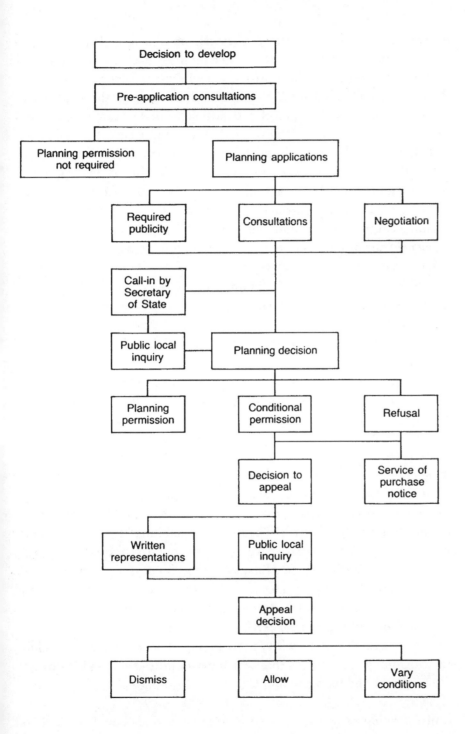

Figure 5.6 The development control process.

density constraints, the use of particular materials, or landscaping. A planning application by ARC Roadstone for mineral extraction in Suffolk resulted in a condition for positive reinstatement being applied. The West Stowe Country Park (Chapter 4) was created by the imaginative use of these exhausted gravel pits which were flooded to provide a water-based recreational facility. Had this type of condition not been included, the area could potentially have been left to resemble the surface of the moon, pitted with craters, a scarred landscape unattractive to the eye and potentially dangerous to the body. Today West Stowe is an important local tourist attraction, reflecting the increasing trend for planning authorities to ensure that their land resources are used not only efficiently but in a manner that accords with environmental concern and public need.

The appropriateness of planning conditions is an issue that has frequently been addressed by planning case law over the years. Planning permissions normally last for a period of 5 years, although where reserved matters are identified these must be agreed within 3 years of approval.

Developers who are unhappy with planning decisions have a right to challenge through the appeal system and ultimately through the courts. Often, however, it is a matter of negotiation and compromise to reflect policy needs of the authority whilst maximizing a financial benefit to the developer. A resubmission of a revised application, or perhaps an agreement or obligation between developer and local authority, can often bring about a suitable result for all the parties.

For example, an unsuccessful planning application for a residential scheme in Dorridge, West Midlands, was resubmitted to include more low-cost housing and open space and subsequently received approval from the local authority. In Horsham, West Sussex, a planning agreement for a road scheme to allow the release of industrial land potential was negotiated between the developer and local authority.

In Scotland the Scottish Office is the central government department with overall responsibility for planning. The structure of development planning is similar to that which exists in England and Wales but with certain administrative and legislative differences.

DEVELOPMENT IN AN INTERNATIONAL CONTEXT

Whilst development may occur to generate economic benefit, sustain or enhance social well-being or perhaps satisfy political ideologies, it is affected by numerous factors which vary from country to country across the world.

The investment potential of property and hence its development is influenced by:

- Social and cultural factors
- Property markets and trading barriers
- Property finance
- Planning systems
- Lease structures and land ownership
- Taxation.

Property professionals vary in terms of their practices and standards and so there is a multiplicity of organizations and diversity of roles in existence worldwide.

It is particularly important when developing in a foreign country to understand and work within the culture of that country. 'Language is not necessarily the issue, but it is important to conduct business their way.'[4] Some countries, for example Sweden, may have higher standards in terms of space allocation or environmental considerations, and developers must therefore reflect these differences in order to compete in the marketplace. Punctuality and politeness are particularly important considerations for business in many countries like Japan and Malaysia and a lack of respect for such social niceties can result in failed business deals.

SOCIAL AND CULTURAL FACTORS

The removal of trading barriers to investments has opened up potential opportunities to developers to go to locations such as Eastern Europe and Russia whilst inward investment into the EU comes from North America, Japan and the Far East. The free movement of capital across world markets has meant that although international growth may benefit a business in the UK (or elsewhere) it is also more susceptible to world recession. Throughout the world, property markets vary dramatically in their level of sophistication. The UK has a well-established property market which has considerable involvement from the financial institutions and ease of trading, and government intervention is kept to a minimum. Many of the European markets and those of the world's developing countries are still in an embryonic stage and their development will be influenced by various players but in particular by financiers, central or local governments and property professionals.

PROPERTY MARKETS AND TRADING BARRIERS

PROPERTY FINANCES

Funding of property development varies considerably from one country to another. In the UK some property developers may try to finance their own schemes, perhaps using profits from previous ventures, but generally pension funds, insurance companies and banks provide the vast majority of funding. Banks tend to provide the bulk of property finance in France and the Netherlands and in some countries like Germany funding may come from non-institutional corporations like breweries.[5] The establishment of a single market in the EU would facilitate the movement of finance from one country to another and some merging of lending institutions has already occurred. Pension funds now have the freedom to invest throughout Europe and hence the property market is becoming directly affected by EU legislation.

The fees charged by agents for property transactions vary quite dramatically across Europe. In France over 22% of the value of the transaction is charged, compared with around 3% in the UK, and this clearly has an influence on investment decisions.

PLANNING SYSTEMS

In general, planning systems both enable and control development activity, but there is tremendous variation in planning practice and organization across Europe with different levels of central and local government involvement in the decision-making process.

The system in Britain is relatively sophisticated and efficient, with planning decisions based on Development Plans occurring within clearly laid down time scales. In Italy delays are relatively common, with local politics generating conflict and indecision. Countries like Portugal and Greece have yet to develop a sophisticated planning system. The Germanic federal system of government results in local control and hence tighter controlled development.[6] In Berlin, developers frequently complain of delays, with application to completion of a project taking a minimum of 5 years. Planning policies that do exist, whether they be at national, regional or local level, will affect demand and supply of property and property values may therefore be influenced by the ease with which permission to develop is obtained.

If one considers the control of retail developments throughout Europe, it is evident that there is some variation in policy but all countries tend to reinforce the principle of protecting existing town centres and restricting new developments (whether in town or out of town). Until the early 1990s the UK had perhaps one of the more relaxed attitudes towards retail development and there are numerous examples of schemes developing both in town and out of town. These include the

Merry Hill centre at Dudley, St David's centre at Cardiff and the One Stop Shopping complex in Birmingham. Countries like Germany, the Netherlands and Belgium have much tighter controls and it is very difficult to obtain approval for out-of-town schemes. Southern European countries, such as Spain and Greece, are still dominated by small shopkeepers who collectively have considerable political influence on planning decisions and hence new major schemes are rare.[7,8]

Before development can occur, it is essential to identify and consult the landowner and to establish the nature of ownership. Whilst this may seem an obvious statement, it is not always an easy task. In many parts of the world, for example South America and Central Europe, establishing the ownership of title of land or a property can be problematic. Differences often exist in the form of land registration and proof of title, and patterns of ownership vary. In Germany, where a system of registration is now being introduced individual ownership predominates; whilst in the UK much of the property is owned by institutional investors and the landed gentry.

    Lease terms differ substantially from one country to another with the less sophisticated markets tending to operate with relatively short leases; for example, one year in Portugal for commercial leases. This compares with 25 years in the UK. Much of European law favours the tenant and hence will restrict the growth of a property investment market. Many countries, like France and Italy, give an automatic right to renew at the end of the term and premiums are charged by outgoing tenants to new occupiers for the benefit of taking on a low rent which is relatively secure.[9]

LEASE STRUCTURES AND LAND OWNERSHIP

Across Europe a range of taxes exist that may influence developments. A study by Arthur Anderson and Nabarro Nathenson in 1991 revealed that problems with taxation and legal systems frequently presented a substantial obstacle to future property investment (or development).[10] For example, in 1994 Value Added Tax (VAT) varied across Europe by more than 5% between the member states and local taxes varied between cities. In France a tax is payable on building and on business activity, whereas the UK operates a Business Rate based on property value. Whilst European harmonization may be the ultimate aim, it is likely to be the next millenium before tax structures are brought into line and hence the impact of taxation on investment returns and on development decisions will continue to be a major consideration.

TAXATION

Table 5.1 Leases

	Length (years)	Tenure	Rent indexed to	Rent review to market level
Belgium	9	3 renewals	annual inflation	yes at renewal
*France***	9	Legal right to renew	cost of building at agreed intervals	no – level set by govt. coefficient at renewal
Germany	10	No right to renew	inflation at agreed trigger	rare
Italy	6	Legal right to renew	75% of annual inflation	no
Netherlands	5–10	Legal right to continue after 5 yrs	annual inflation	by agreement at renewal
Portugal	1	Legal right to renew	annual inflation	no
Spain pre-1985	3–10	Legal right to renew	annual inflation/ none	no
Spain post-1985	1–10	No right to renew	annual inflation	no
UK	25	Legal right to renew	none	every 5 years*

* upwards only
** a 12 year term removes the right to renew and allows renewals at market rent

WORKPIECE 5.5

LAND REGISTRATION

What is registration of title?
In England and Wales, what is the role of the land registry?
Using a country of your own choice, identify the terms of a typical commercial lease.

PROPERTY PROFESSIONALS' PRACTICES AND STANDARDS

Property professionals play a significant role in acquisition and disposal of land or property, but often qualifications obtained in one country will not allow practice in another. In Britain the Royal Institution of Chartered Surveyors (RICS) has a well-developed structure for education and training but to practise as a real estate agent in the Netherlands or Spain requires further special qualification. There is still a huge variation in the qualification of property professionals world-wide. In Europe, property expertise tends to be more of a broking nature and is dealt with by lawyers, accountants, architects or engineers. The EU Directive on Mutual Recognition of Professional Diplomas (1990) attempted to promote the mobility of labour amongst professionals but, despite lobbying by the RICS, there is little sign of its professional qualifications being recognized.

In addition to variations in education and training amongst European property professionals, there are also differences in professional practises. For example, different approaches apply to the measurement of buildings which can result in details on floor areas and spaces per square metre being difficult to compare. (The UK practice of excluding service ducts and internal columns gives floor areas 17% less than in Belgium and 10% less than in France.) In some countries buildings may not actually be measured for a property transaction as details are obtained from leases (Sweden), official computer (Holland) or from reported measurements to the local authority (Denmark).[11]

The different approach to area measurement is often reflected in the internal design features of many continental buildings. Air-conditioning is not necessarily placed in ceilings and false floors are rare, with heating, cooling and power features located in casing around the perimeter of rooms. Fire regulations also influence design considerations. 'Germany requires a central fire resisting corridor to be provided down the spine of all its buildings.'[12]

EU-influenced legislation on health and safety and on environment issues (as well as other areas) applies to all member states but its enforcement is variable. Property (both new and old) over time will be required to comply with these legislative provisions and this will provide both an interesting and expensive challenge for landlords, tenants, managers and owners alike. The skills required by property managers will continue to expand and so perhaps will the management cost unless management techniques can be developed further.

Function and efficiency are clearly fundamental issues for buildings in mainland Europe, with the emphasis on ease of maintenance and lower costs. In many cases it is evident that short lease patterns encourage landlords to ensure that buildings are managed well so that when properties become available they attract maximum interest.

Service charges will range from approximately 12% of rent payable

**DESIGN AND
MANAGEMENT**

in countries like France to 25% in Spain (1994 levels). These are relatively constant and hence if rental levels fall they will form an increasingly higher proportion of the net rent.

The nature of employment, particularly in the office sector, is changing due to technology and in the future it is likely that companies will need fewer employees to work at the office. Smaller office units will therefore be required and perhaps firms will no longer see the necessity for the so-called 'head office'. Such dramatic changes will mean far fewer occupiers will sign up for long leases and the days of the major space users in cities will be a thing of the past.[8]

SUMMARY

The development of landscape and townscape has seen major changes over the centuries. The costs and benefits of developments have increased dramatically, not merely in economic terms, but also in social and environmental terms.

The diverse and complex nature of development will always require a large number of 'players'. Controls over the process have become increasingly sophisticated over the years.

Changing political, religious and cultural attitudes in many parts of the world have opened up new opportunities for investment and development and there is a continuous need for information and for understanding to be expanded to allow this potential to be realized.

Through this chapter we have:

● explored how development has taken place in the UK;
● looked at the roles of the various 'players' in the development process;
● examined the broad basis of development control in the UK;
● considered some of the factors influencing development decisions in the UK and other countries.

KEY CONCEPTS

● Development of landscape and townscape has evolved over the centuries.
● Control has shifted from private to public control.
● The increased scale and complexity of development activity has necessitated the introduction of formal control to ensure that adequate consideration is given to issues of environment, quality, efficiency, performance and safety for individuals and the community at large.

- The development process involves a wide variety of players.
- Development, whilst frequently associated with profit, often makes a significant contribution to quality of the urban environment.
- Some development is non-profit making.
- Development occurs due to the needs and demands of society or the speculation of the developer.
- Development as an activity follows a series of stages, many of which run concurrently rather than in sequence.
- Development and the investment potential of property across the world are affected by numerous factors.

REFERENCES

1. Moore, V. (1992) *A practical approach to Planning Law*, Blackstone Press.
2. Burke, G. (1971) *Towns in the Making*, Arnold.
3. Cadman, D. and Austin Crowe, L. (1991) *Property Development*. E & FN Spon.
4. Perrin, R. (1992) French landing. *Estates Times Europe, European Review* 6 March 1992.
5. Estates Europe (1992) Country Survey: Germany. *The European Property Newsletter*, Match, Vol. 1, No. 1, March 1992.
6. Kenzle, O. (1992) 21st Century arrival. *Estates Times, European Review*, 23 October.
7. Rald, Linbeerk van (1992) Guilder goslow. *Estates Times, European Review*, 5 March, p.24.
8. Estates Europe (1993) Survey: Shopping centres. *The European Property Newsletter*, October, Vol. 2.
9. Centre for European Property Research (1992) *A comparative study of commercial leasing structures in selected European countries, England and the USA*. RICS 1992
10. Anderson, A. and Nathanson, N. (1991) *Building a Stake in Europe*, Investment Property Databank.
11. Wheatcroft, D. (1992) Paper at European Property Conference, Henry Stewart.
12. Warner, M. (1994) Offices with personality. *Estate Times Review*, 4 March, p. 66.

FURTHER READING

Burke, G. (1976) *Townscapes*, Penguin.
DOE (1989) *Planning Control in Western Europe*.

CHAPTER SIX

INFLUENCES ON DESIGN

ANN BURNS

THEME

Traditionally, building methods were related very closely to the local economy and the availability of materials. Buildings could be dated and located in clear geographical and historical contexts. Despite this, styles have swept the world in different civilizations, for example during the Roman Empire or the Norman Conquest. The twentieth century has seen an increasing emphasis on the standardization of building forms and ideas. Sometimes this is because of political concerns and on other occasions may be social or economic. This chapter explores the relationship between the nature of available materials, their utilization and the influence of government on the control of buildings. It uses the architecture of Greece and Rome as a basis for understanding relationships between the social, political and cultural context of buildings and their design and construction and traces the influences of 'building controls' on the design and appearance of buildings in different periods and countries.

OBJECTIVES

At the end of this chapter you should be able to:

● understand ways in which societies develop their controls on buildings;

● understand influences of such controls on the appearance of buildings;

● identify influences of various cultures on the appearance of buildings;

116

- understand some of the reasons why the availability of materials influences the appearance of buildings;

- understand the relationship between buildings and their context.

To some extent the appearance of buildings still relates closely to the local economy and the availability of local materials. Buildings and cities can still be dated and located in clear historical and geographical contexts. For example, the predominant construction material in Scandinavia and parts of Canada is timber. Similarly igloos are built from ice. Cities can be defined by the materials predominantly used in their construction although they may have absorbed many different architectural styles. However, the influence of the availability and utilization of materials cannot be assessed in isolation because the appearance of buildings and the development of cities has also been heavily influenced by a number of other factors, including:

- the desire to build monuments to express superiority, power and ideology;
- the implementation of social and political control;
- the application of design and technology;
- requirements of defence;
- religion;
- economic development and commercial prosperity;
- improved communication and centralization of production;
- design concepts which are reinterpreted by different societies and civilizations at separate points in history.

THE DESIRE TO BUILD MONUMENTS TO EXPRESS SUPERIORITY, POWER AND IDEOLOGY

Throughout history, governments and powerful authorities have striven to leave their ideological signature on civilization. Cities and grand structures of dramatic size and proportion have been built as monuments to intellectual or military superiority and power. A series of powerful authorities, whether Greek, Roman, nineteenth century local authorities in Britain or modern multi-national companies have constructed buildings and cities which reflect their ideology.

In modern cities, huge uncompromising multi-storey blocks of steel and glass have been built which dominate the cityscape, showing little regard for or empathy with the local surroundings. Such monuments to power and prestige reflect the nature of the modern business world and the ideology of money and big business.

The Greeks created buildings to stand as monuments to their intellect and the achievements of their civilization. The Greek architectural orders of Doric, Ionic and later Corinthian which defined the appearance of most buildings were designed not only as conventional structural systems but almost as a geometric exercise taken to its highest perfection to express their intellectual superiority.

Figure 6.1 Birmingham Town Hall, a nineteenth century 'Greek' temple. (Tom Muir.)

The Greek temple form was never radically changed: any development is considered intelligent refinement. The strict use of proportions transmitted the template design from architect to architect in many different cities. It can be argued that Greek temple architecture has little to do with either structure or function. The Greeks considered themselves to be a highly intelligent race and built monuments to express their superiority for posterity.

Such buildings can be seen as standardized building forms replicated across the world with little or no relation to the physical context in which they were then placed. But what drove the creation of these

CLASSICAL ORDERS

Individually or in groups, can you think of a village, town or city where no reference to the orders of classical architecture can be found at all?

If you have been able to come up with three places

where there is no reference to these orders, then identify four reasons why.

If you have not been able to think of three places, or you have found it difficult, explain why.

monuments? Was it the desire to express power and superiority or was it ideologically driven? Probably the answer is a combination of both these and other factors.

Unlike the Greeks, the Romans wanted to express their military prowess and imperial pride rather than their intellect. Roman imperialism was expressed in the reconstruction of each new conquest as the empire expanded.

Where the Romans imposed their style on the existing buildings of the previous culture as a mark of conquest, an eclectic mix and match of styles and traditions has resulted. Roman styles of appearance and planning were imposed on cities throughout the empire regardless of existing local culture or surroundings. Each conquest was sealed with a symbol of Roman superiority.

> The Roman virtually invented the capital city. Rome itself was the first of a long line culminating in Vienna and Paris. With that outward expression of imperialism came also into art the 'grand manner' – the formal axis, the triumphal arch, the culminating palace, the avenue, the fountains and all the symmetrical attributes of power and vanity.[1]

Symbols of Roman superiority were built across the empire and each conqueror in turn left their own mark on cities. Cities were built to stand as monuments to the achievements of Roman civilization. Each was based on a standard plan which reflected control and power.

What was the thinking behind Roman town planning? The principal purpose as the empire expanded was to provide a network of linked colonies that could function as military units in the case of war.[2]

New settlements were logically planned as military camps so they could function in this manner. The Romans adapted the Greek gridiron arrangement so that each settlement could be organized as a military camp if required. This type of regimented, logical planning appealed to the Roman military mind. Examples include Cosa (Ansedonia) on the Tuscan Coast and Marzabotto near Bologna. Cosa clearly shows how regimented the settlements were. The place is enclosed by a high wall built to house a garrison if necessary and divided by a series of streets and perpendicular cross streets with gates at the ends of the two main thoroughfares. This form of standard plan helped travelling garrisons to locate themselves quickly and efficiently so that they were ready to fight, if necessary.

In their early years places like this would have been sensitive to the threat of attack. However when this threat subsided these early military settlements developed into more domestic colonies which grew out of the already established regimental town planning approach. Palmyra is a good example; planned as a military camp, it then developed and eventually evolved into a wealthy Roman town.

Monuments expressing power, superiority and ideology have been built by successive civilizations, throughout history. Modern conquerors, such as multinational businesses, also build symbols to their power and prestige.

SOCIAL/POLITICAL CONTROL

Throughout history, governments have achieved a degree of social and political control through intervention in the planning and designing of buildings and cities.

The Romans succeeded in uniting their empire with its diverse societies and peoples without excessive subjugation, through the application of their urban systems of town planning.

> Rome found herself the political mistress of a kalideoscope of peoples covering every shade of the civilized spectrum. It was her great achievement that ... she did succeed in welding this heterogeneous assortment into a body politic within which all the participants could feel themselves to be in some real sense Roman.[3]

The imposition of Roman urban administration throughout the empire's colonies provided an effective framework for development and social control. Wherever an appropriate urban system did not exist they created a blueprint of roads, towns and public buildings to form a social framework which could be strictly monitored and controlled.

What features characterized a typical colony? A good example is Augustua Raurica (Basle). There the streets were laid out in a grid of rectangular units. Private and public buildings were developed within this practical although arguably unimaginative layout. The concept of the provision of public buildings was widely introduced by the Romans. Public buildings specifically for commerce, religion and leisure were planned into the Roman city to centralize social activity. A large forum and a basilica, a theatre and a large market were typically grouped together centrally, usually divided by the main route through the town. The forum was a central space surrounded by buildings in which the population assembled to conduct their official and religious affairs. The basilica was a law court and commercial centre. Both functioned as social meeting places. The provision of such centres and public amenities created an environment on which the Romans could impose an element of social control. Although such a definitive layout dictated the activity, growth and expansion of cities, it also gave towns and their citizens a sense of unity.

Each of these social building types had their own distinctive style and appearance. The basilica in particular was built to a formula which was replicated across the empire. Standardized designs for public buildings were recognized as the centre of social activity in towns and cities.

Although built to a formula, the appearance of such public buildings was also determined by the availability of materials and building skills. With the changing nature of local materials and skills each new town would have been a regional interpretation of the original idea.

How have other periods differed in their approach to the organization and planning of public buildings?

WORKPIECE 6.2

STYLE AND PLACE

Either individually or in groups, discuss the different styles and periods of buildings in the place you are in. Are there examples of buildings from other periods? Which do you consider to be more attractive – buildings which reflect historical styles or modern buildings? Why? Identify three buildings from three different periods (e.g. mediaeval, Victorian and modern). Discuss the answers to the following questions:

● What are their similarities and differences?
● How have local materials affected their design?
● What statutory controls do you think were in force when each was constructed?

Mediaeval towns and villages in Britain reflected a more organic approach to social organizations.[4] This was true of vernacular architecture in many different countries. However, when governments have embarked on the renewal of major public buildings, concepts relating back to Roman town planning can still be identified. Classical architecture and the use of the orders, the grouping of large buildings around formal public spaces and the gridiron layout of streets have heavily influenced the layout of towns and cities throughout the last two thousand years. Paris, Washington DC, parts of London, New Delhi and San Francisco are just a few places where these ideas can be seen.

THE APPLICATION OF DESIGN AND TECHNOLOGY

The development of technology and its application to solve a practical or technical problem has dramatically altered the appearance of buildings and cities from the Roman age to the twentieth century. Technology has not only solved complex problems but also pushed back the boundaries of the building process. Seemingly impossible aims have been achieved and new concepts made possible as a result of finding new ways to use materials and components in the construction of buildings and the planning of cities.

The Romans were challenged by the practical problems of, firstly, building arches to span greater distances and, secondly, accommodating large numbers of people in one place to worship, trade or spectate. The application of primitive technology to solve these problems resulted in the development of concrete as a building material. The Romans revolutionized building as a result. The definitive style and appearance of Roman architecture was defined by the use of concrete as a material.

Roman concrete consisted of a clean, finely pulverized, dark red volcanic earth which was mixed in a kiln with limestone. This 'quicklime' was then poured over an aggregate consisting of either chips or waste stone, selected depending on the purpose for which it would be used. The resulting material was a compact, monolithic, highly cohesive mass which set very hard even when submerged in water. It was not until the discovery of Portland cement in the nineteenth century, over 2000 years later, that a better binding material was developed. The domes and arches designed by the Romans were made practical as a result of the properties of this new material.

The introduction of concrete made it possible to design and build structural components of revolutionary dimensions and proportions changing the entire appearance of buildings. Early Greek and Roman arches had been relatively unambitious without the knowledge of concrete. The structural properties of concrete, which absorbed the internal stresses, enabled the Romans to build arches that could span greater distances and support greater structures.

The Aemilian Portico at Rome offers a good example. It consisted of a market hall with four parallel aisles crossed by barrel vaulted trancepts supported on a large number of arches. The entire structure was made possible by using concrete. The floor was of concrete which was stepped to adjust to the rising levels of the ground covered by irregular stones. The arches were constructed by pouring liquid concrete over timber-framed structures which were then removed once the concrete had begun to harden. This is exactly the same way that concrete is used with timber shoring or formwork in modern construction.

There are numerous examples of buildings which would not have been possible without the application of concrete. However, the most significant outcome of the development of concrete is the change in the appearance of buildings as a result of the application of design and technology to solve the problem of accommodating large numbers of people in one place.

The development of concrete enabled the evolution of other structural components. The barrel vault evolved as a longitudinal extension of the arch. Revolutionary structures were now made possible. The complex four-storey circular structure of the Flavian amphitheatre in Rome, the Colosseum, is supported by concrete arch-bearing piers and barrel vaults. The columns are merely decoration. Such a structure was only possible with the development of concrete.

The development of technology in the Roman age not only dramatically changed the appearance of buildings but also had a dramatic effect on the concept of architecture as a whole. The basilica, with its improved concrete structure, enabled large numbers of people to assemble comfortably in one place. As a result buildings such as the Basilica of Maxentius (AD 306–312) or the basilica at Pompeii (*ca*. 120 BC) began to function as the 'social exchange' central to Roman society. The building was seen to be a function of society rather than a form of shelter. This adjusted perception is clearly seen in the Pantheon (reconstructed in AD 117–138). The entrance is through a huge colonnaded portico leading into a central space capped with a dome 43.5 m high with a radius of approximately 20 m. It is based on a sphere where the height of the walls is equal to the radius of the dome. The dome is constructed of brick-faced concrete 6 m thick with rectangular recesses, thereby lightening the concrete structure. The dome exerts no outward pressure on the supporting structure but rests on the walls like a lid. The Pantheon had been designed as a building for great numbers of people to assemble in as a congregation under the huge dome.

Figure 6.2 The Pantheon in Rome, a source for many later buildings. (Peter Maddern.)

The development of technology resulting in the evolution of concrete had 'created an architecture in which the decisive factor was no longer the solid masonry but the space it enclosed. And in the process, this revolutionary material had helped to alter religious and social customs'.[5]

In the nineteenth and twentieth centuries, technology and experimentation with materials have pushed the boundaries of the building process forward. New materials, such as iron, steel and glass in the nineteenth century and plastic, reinforced plastic, reinforced concrete, chipboard and plywood in the twentieth century, have generated new building types and structures.

Traditional materials have also evolved as both new and old materials have been exploited to their design limits and matched together. This application of technology has made the construction of new building types possible.

The Pantheon exemplified changes in society and the building process. Are there examples of modern structures which have done the same? In the nineteenth century the Crystal Palace designed by Joseph Paxton for the Great Exhibition of 1851 in London reflected the nature of Great Britain as a trading nation and altered people's perception of

Figure 6.3 A typical townscape in England (Bury St Edmunds) constructed over a period of more than 300 years. Note how many buildings use classical details. (David Chapman.)

the use of glass and cast iron. Twentieth century structures like the suspension bridge across the Bosphorus and the tunnel under the English Channel – the world's busiest shipping lane – are radically changing patterns of mobility and transport. Innovative buildings like the Pompidou Centre in Paris, the Hong Kong and Shanghai Bank in Hong Kong and the Munich Stadium have made us think again about how to accommodate large numbers of people in one place either for work purposes or to enjoy leisure and sport. The problem of how to create places of assembly is as important to modern society as it was to Rome.

WORKPIECE 6.3

LOCAL BUILDINGS

Either by taking a walk around your locality, or by discussing your locality in a group with other people, list six buildings which use the classical orders in some way. Answer the following questions:

● What are the variations between the different orders used?

● In what period were the buildings built?
● Why do you think these buildings use the classical orders?
● Do you believe we should still be using these orders today?

THE REQUIREMENTS OF DEFENCE

Protection of a community has been a priority in the development of any settlement. The requirements of defence have shaped the evolution of towns and cities and often determined their location.

One of the principal purposes of Roman town planning as the empire expanded was to provide a network of linked colonies that could function as military units in the case of war. New settlements were logically planned as military camps so they could function in this manner. We have already discussed one example of a place (Palmyra) that was built as a military settlement but later evolved to become a wealthy town.

The Normans are another example of a society which evolved a particular approach to architecure and building and the requirements of defence as their empire expanded over much of Europe, from England to the Mediterranean and the Middle East. Examples of Norman fortifications, which can be easily recognized for their style and appearance as well as their layout and form, can be found in England, France, Italy and Malta. In a space of 200 years the Normans created an extensive network of colonies and countries. While we now enjoy unravelling and understanding their history, culture, artefacts and designs, for the indigenous people of the period Norman rule imposed radical changes on society and its buildings.

Mediaeval cities were based on the fundamental requirement of protection. Most mediaeval towns and cities originated from a defensive settlement or castle which may have included Norman structures. The planning and building of castles were a direct result of the necessities of defence. The castle functioned not only as a position of defence but also as a fortified habitation for the local community.

RELIGION

The power, wealth and influence of the Church through history has resulted in new architectural developments at different periods. Vast financial and human resources have been pooled together by the Church for the construction of places of worship. Each of the numerous varieties of different religions at different periods of history have made their contributions.

In Britain, the Church played an active part in destroying the axial streets of the Roman layout and re-established local traditions. The requirements of the Church were enough to disregard Roman planning completely if necessary. For example, the expansion of the Norman church at Lincoln resulted in an irregular walled close which is partly in and partly out of the original limits of the Roman colony.

During the Middle Ages the Church became increasingly powerful, manifesting its power by building new churches and cathedrals as monuments. These became the most important buildings in a community and represented local traditions. The church was also the symbol of the afterlife and as such was carefully maintained and built from the best local materials.

Economic development has acted as a catalyst in the development of cities. As governments or local economies have experienced periods of commercial prosperity, cities have expanded with the increase of trade. During periods of material wealth and prosperity, design details of buildings have changed dramatically. The rate and nature of development has been defined by the level of commercial prosperity.

How can this be seen in the development of mediaeval towns and cities? In towns which were profiting from trade, new streets were being formed outside the ancient fortifications. Such spontaneous growth was controlled primarily by local topography. As trade increased new towns, such as St Albans, were planned as trading centres. Such places were built around a long triangular marketplace formed by widening the main road through the town or village. The marketplace became the nucleus of commercial activity. The frontages on this road were divided up into lots to be rented by prospective traders. These lots were occupied by market stalls which gradually became permanent structures and eventually shops and houses.

As trade increased, new streets and plots of land were added to existing towns or villages to establish new trading communities. Completely new settlements were created on previously uninhabited sites. As trade developed, these sites rapidly expanded to accommodate increasing numbers of potential traders. In some areas whole new towns were created as trade centres. The impact of trade and commerce was so significant that the definition of 'cities' as opposed to towns and villages was determined by the presence of merchants and tradesmen.

The impact of trade and commerce on the appearance of buildings is demonstrated in cities such as Chester. Town houses were tightly packed together, making use of every available lettable space facing on to the street. Usually they were timber-framed buildings with a narrow frontage and gabled street elevation. The fronts of houses on the main streets were occupied by active workshops where the merchants or traders only required enough space to practise their trade. As a result there was an abundance of tightly packed individual shop units. If there was any space between houses, then as trade increased it became occupied by temporary stalls which in turn became permanent structures attached to the houses. Eventually the fronts of the houses were brought forward to take in the stalls. This had the effect of narrowing the street by 4–5 ft on either side, and creating a covered walkway at first floor level known as a 'row'. These became characteristic features of prosperous commercial cities.

The impact of commerce in such areas can be measured by the number of streets associated with individual trades. Individual trades must also have had their influence on the appearance of the frontages of their shop units or workshops. As merchants became more successful, their houses and frontages would express wealth. The more successful merchants would build larger houses set back from the street with a gateway as an indication of their commercial success.

Economic development and the potential profits of commerce clearly influenced the evolution of towns into cities. The economics of investing in the construction of shops took priority over any formal town planning and motivated the development of cities. There were no formal requirements to invest large amounts of capital to provide new layouts complete with streets, specified marketplaces and residential plots. As a result there was little deliberate planning or concern for environmental conditions in such areas of towns. Comparisons can be made between the mediaeval and the rapidly developing modern Third World city.

Building regulations and by-laws did not exist as such, but as places become more crowded and environmental health problems were identified, the beginnings of building regulations emerged. A good example of the introduction of an early regulation was the requirement to cantilever out the upper levels of houses over streets, so that waste could be thrown directly into the middle of the road, rather than poured on to passers-by immediately below the window. This regulation affected the visual appearance of buildings and can be seen in examples of half-timbered houses that have survived.

In the Western world statutory controls over buildings have grown dramatically in the last 100 years. Floor-to-ceiling heights, foundations, insulation, condensation problems and ventilation are just a few of the topics covered in the UK building regulations. These controls have a direct bearing on the use of materials in buildings and their appearance.

WORKPIECE 6.4

REGULATIONS

Taking the building you are in as an example, list the building and/or planning regulations that you believe would have affected its layout and visual appearance.

WORKPIECE 6.5

VISUAL CHARACTERISTICS

Identify one modern building you know.
  List its main visual characteristics.
  Discuss how these have been influenced by statutory regulations such as building regulations or planning permission.

IMPROVED COMMUNICATIONS AND CENTRALIZATION OF PRODUCTION

The twentieth century has experienced dramatically improved communications and transport. This has clearly facilitated the more effective distribution of building materials. Production has been centralized. Materials that were once available only in their area of origin are now widely available nationally and indeed internationally. Inevitably, building forms and styles have become increasingly standardized. Although standardized forms have spread rapidly, traditional styles have evolved as regional interpretations.

The increased availability of standard building materials has also led to greater standardization of town planning. This can be seen in the planning of new towns in both developing and developed countries. Standard planning models have emerged as the most effective method of accommodating large numbers of people in new towns.

Canberra, Brazilia and Chandigrah are three examples of international cities designed specifically to solve the perceived needs of society at the time of their creation and which were generated by central government concerns. Consistent themes have run through the organization and planning of new towns and cities across the world, including for example:

● the creation of 'neighbourhoods';
● the promotion of good traffic management;
● the grouping of housing, medical and commercial buildings.

These ideas have already been identified in Chapter 4 and discussed in Chapter 5.

SUMMARY

Throughout history, governments and authorities have striven to leave their ideological signature on civilization. Cities and structures of dramatic size and proportion have been built as monuments to intellectual or military superiority and to express ideology and power.

Governments have achieved a degree of social and political control through intervention in the planning and designing of buildings and cities.

The development technology and its application to solve a practical or technical problem has dramatically altered the appearance of buildings and the development of cities. Seemingly impossible aims have been achieved and new concepts made possible as a result of finding new ways to use materials and components in the construction of buildings.

Protection of a community has been a priority in the development of any settlement, whether it is a small town or a capital city. The requirements of defence have shaped the evolution of towns and cities and often determined their location.

The power, wealth and influence of the religious organizations have throughout history resulted in new architectural developments and the pooling of vast human and physical resources to construct places of worship.

Economic development has acted as a catalyst in the development of cities. As governments or local economies have experienced periods of commercial prosperity, cities have expanded with the increase of trade.

The design and detailing of buildings have been dramatically developed either in function or appearance during periods of material wealth and prosperity. The rate and nature of development has been defined by the level of commercial prosperity.

The increasing standardization of planning, building and development processes is an important issue and something that affects many people in their daily lives. The growth of international trade coupled with this standardization is creating major challenges. How can regional identities and cultures be maintained or enhanced while encouraging global stability and peace?

Society has controlled the quality of buildings through the introduction of statutory regulations and requirements.

Improved communications have clearly facilitated the more effective distribution of building materials. Production has become more centralized. Materials that were once only available in their area of origin are now widely available nationally and indeed internationally. Inevitably, building forms and styles have become increasingly standardized, particularly as planning processes have become more international. Although standardization has spread rapidly, traditional styles have also evolved. However, there is an increasing need to recognize local, regional and national needs in the development process.

The appearance of buildings has been affected by:

- the availability of materials;
- the desire to build monuments to express superiority, power and ideology;
- the implementation of social and political control;
- the application of design and technology;
- the requirements of defence;
- the power and influence of religion;
- economic development and commercial prosperity;
- legislation and statutory building controls;
- improved communications which have led to standardized buildings and town planning.

1. Furneaux Jordan, R. (1971) *Concise History of Western Architecture*, Thames and Hudson.
2. Salway, P. (1993) *Oxford Illustrated History of Roman Britain*, Oxford University Press.
3. Boethius, A. and Ward Perkins, J.B. (1970) *Etruscan and Roman Architecture*, Penguin.
4. Poole, A. L. (1958) *Mediaeval England*, Vols 1 and 2, Oxford University Press.
5. Guedes, P. (1979) *MacMillan Encyclopaedia of Architecture and Technological Change*, MacMillan.

Fletcher, Sir Bannister (1993) *History of Architecture*, Butterworth–Heinemann.
Fleming, J., Honour, H. and Pevsner, N. (1985) *Dictionary of Architecture*, Penguin.

PART THREE

THE DESIGN AND CONSTRUCTION OF BUILDINGS

CONCEPTS OF STRUCTURE AND SPACE

CHAPTER SEVEN

ADRIAN NAPPER

THEME

Without structure, buildings would collapse. All built environment professionals should therefore have an understanding of the fundamental principles of structure and their relative impact. Such a grounding should be a sound basis for future specialists in this field as well as an essential brief to those who will engage primarily in non-construction issues. This chapter provides a lively synopsis of structural types and forms illustrated with examples from a variety of countries and historical contents. It touches on the impact of large-scale structures in the environment (for example, dams) but only as an indicator of the scale of intervention humans have sought to achieve.

OBJECTIVES

At the end of this chapter you should be able to:

● understand the range of structural concepts available today;

● recognize their visual characteristics and spatial implications;

● be able to sum up the relative merits of different concepts and systems;

● be able to relate them to a range of building projects;

● understand relationships between structure, services and building form with reference to a variety of user and client requirements.

INTRODUCTION

Until about 150 years ago all building structures were designed without the benefit of any engineering mathematics. Domes spanning 30 m like the Pantheon in Rome, Gothic cathedrals like Amiens 40 m high and palaces like Blenheim all managed to stand up without assistance from mathematics. They were overwhelmingly made from the traditional structural materials – stone, brick and timber – and relied upon experience and convention and upon clients not being too concerned about failures. For example, Beauvais Cathedral collapsed and was rebuilt twice.

The nineteenth century saw the development of two new structural materials: iron alloys (i.e. cast iron, wrought iron and steel) and reinforced concrete. The same period also saw the introduction of ways of using numbers to describe roughly how structures worked. These allowed designers to predict how new and innovative structures would perform. Professional engineers were expected to guarantee that their structures would not fail. Today society expects the structures of their buildings to be safe. It also expects that they will be 'efficient', that is to say they will not use more resources than are necessary.

To design safe and efficient structures it is necessary to understand how they work. What are the ideas and concepts behind different structures and forms? In this chapter we shall be discussing some detailed technical concepts but in layman's language. Where should we start?

GRAVITY, OR KEEPING ON BOARD

As well as whirling round the sun, our planet is also spinning on its axis at a speed of 28 000 miles every 24 hours. To stay at rest on the surface of the Earth every object has to be kept in place by a number of force systems, notably the force of gravity.

Gravity is a rather well worked out means of keeping objects in equilibrium and it is just the right size so that we are neither flung out into space nor crushed down into the ground. Isaac Newton showed that every object is pulled down towards the centre of the earth. The size of the pull is directly proportional to the 'mass' of the object and varies with its distance from the centre of the earth. **Mass** is the amount of material in a body.

In physics you may have learnt that gravitational pull is more at the Poles than at the Equator. While this may be interesting for the scientist, it is irrelevant for the engineering designer. When designing engineering structures it is important to understand the scientific theories that describe the way nature works but it is also sensible to simplify them and to disregard refinements that will not have a measurable influence on relatively crude building structures. For structures on earth, then, engineers assume that all objects are pulled downwards by a force that is proportional to its mass. This force is called the **'weight'** of the object.

A force is a **'vector'** which means it has size, direction and a point of application. It can be represented by a line. The line has length, which represents size and direction and can be thought of as acting at a particular point.

The size of a force can be measured by multiplying the mass by the acceleration with which it would move. **Acceleration** is the rate of change of speed. The acceleration of gravity is taken to be $9.81 \, \mathrm{m \, s^2}$.

These principles are important if we are to understand the nature of forces that affect buildings and the way they stand up. Let us take this further by exploring the human form as a structural system.

Structural action is not an 'abstract' phenomenon like electricity which can only be appreciated by studying measuring devices. Every human being is a structural system and with our bones and muscles and tendons we balance forces all the time.

Imagine you are holding a 10 kg bag of potatoes out at arm's length. If you let the bag go, it will fall towards the centre of the earth, accelerating as it falls. If you hang on to it, you prevent it falling and apply to the potatoes a supporting force equal and opposite to its weight. Equilibrium is achieved if the upward support from your hand exactly balances the downward pull of gravity. This upward force has to be transferred through your wrist, arm, elbow, shoulder, body and through your feet to whatever you are standing on. If you happen to be standing on a fragile or rickety chair, it is possible that the extra force created by the weight of the potatoes could cause it to collapse or fall over. Similarly, any one of the parts of your body might decide that the effort was too much and give up.

In exactly the same way the different parts of the building have to transfer forces applied to them from one part to another and eventually all forces have to be transferred through the foundations and into the ground. The ground also has to be able to establish an equilibrium condition between forces that act upon it and its own capacity to push back against those forces.

In the end all forces generated by gravity have to be resisted by the earth's crust. Otherwise they would just keep going on to the centre of the earth.

A PERSON AS A STRUCTURAL SYSTEM

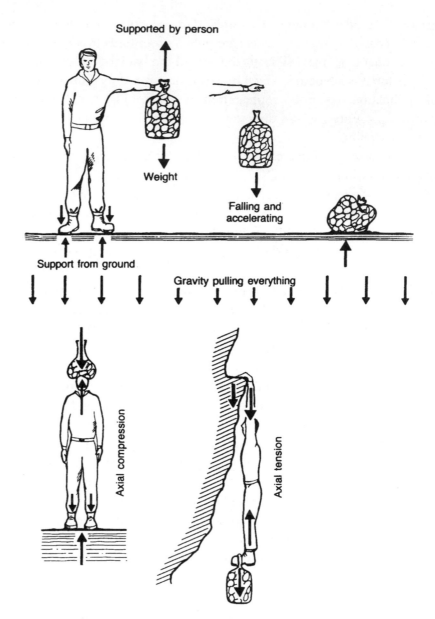

Figure 7.1 A person as a structural system.

The mechanisms by which the body transfers forces from hand to foot etc. are the same as the ones buildings use to transfer forces from roof to foundation via floors and walls, beams and columns. There are the four basic mechanisms for transferring forces: compression, tension, bending and shear.

BODY AS STRUCTURE

Considering your body as a 'structure' and a 10 kg bag of potatoes as a 'load', explore different configurations of your body which will transfer the weight of the potatoes through your body into the ground.

For example, put your feet together and put your left arm by your side; then, holding the potatoes in your right hand, put them as far away from your body as you can. Draw a diagram of your structure and indicate where your body structure is working the hardest and which parts are in bending and which in compression.

Change the configuration of your body to make the passage of the forces through your body easier.

Make your body into a 'bridge' spanning between two chairs.

Suspend the load from your finger.

Stand on one leg and support the 'load' from your free foot.

Draw diagrams of each body form indicating the stress points and the axes of symmetry.

LOADS AND SUPPORTS

Survey the building that you are in and try to identify the 'route' by which the loads are transferred into the ground. Try to find out:

● What supports the roof?
● Are there any columns and how far apart are they?
● Do they connect to the floor?
● Which walls are loadbearing and which are partitions?

● Which parts of the external envelope are structural and how do they relate to the fenestration?

Draw a scale diagram which describes the 'route'.

Discuss whether the structure is clear or hidden and whether the appearance of the structure influences the appreciation of the space.

Find another building which has a contrasting relation between the structure and the appearance.

If you stand upright with the bag of potatoes on your head, you transfer the load by **axial compression.**

If you hang by your fingertip from a rock ledge with a bag of potatoes suspended from your ankles, you are transferring their weight through your body by **axial tension.**

In **tension**, you are being pulled apart and you maintain equilibrium by pulling inwards at each end. In **compression**, you are being squashed together and you maintain equilibrium by pushing outward at your ends.

In buildings, columns, walls and struts are normally in axial compression; ties are in axial tension.

In axial tension and compression the members transferring forces lie in the same direction as the forces. When members are required to transfer forces that are acting at an angle to them, they have to use the property of **bending**.

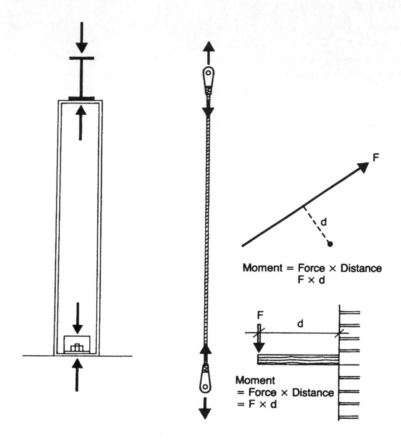

Figure 7.2 Compression, tension and bending.

Human bodies are quite familiar with resisting bending. The shoulder of the arm that is stretched out has to work to keep the arm horizontal. It has to produce what is called a **'moment'**, which is a turning effect to maintain the system in balance. The size of this moment depends on two things:

● the weight of the bag of potatoes (the force generated by gravity on the mass of the potatoes);
● the length of the arm (the distance beween the force and the point where the moment is being considered).

A **bending moment** is the turning effect of a force acting about a point. The size of the bending moment is measured by multiplying the force by the minimum distance between the point and the line of action of the force. Units are force (measured in newtons, N) times distance and are called newton metres (N m).

We are aware of the shoulder acting as a way of resisting a turning effect but the resistance must also apply to every point along the arm. The bones in arms make them stiff, the joint of the elbow can be locked and so each part of the system can resist bending. If arms were made of rubber it would be a different story.

Normal bones are pretty good at resisting bending. They are not flexible (bendy) and are not normally brittle. However, old age or illness can make them brittle, in which case they may not be strong enough to transfer the load. They will not bend – they will snap. This is where **shear** comes in. In shear, parallel planes are displaced in a direction parallel to themselves and tend to slide over each other.

THE BALANCED SEE-SAW

Using the body to describe the transfer of load systems is a way of relating structural action to our own experience. It is necessary to move to the next stage and further relate these systems to the structure of buildings. Before doing so, it is useful to consider how a see-saw works. It is obvious when a see-saw is balanced and when it is not. The rules that apply to a see-saw have to be applied to all structures.

The first rule is that **all vertical forces must balance**. Normally this means that the pull of gravity downwards must be resisted by forces acting upwards. These upward forces are normally generated by the supports to the system, i.e. the foundations. If the downward forces are larger than the upward, the system will disappear into the ground. If the upward forces are bigger than the downward, then the system will rise into the air.

Because gravity is the main force on most buildings, the balancing of upward and downward forces is the principle concern. In fact this is a particular example of the general requirement of equilibrium that forces in any direction must balance.

The second rule is that **the turning effect at every point must balance**, i.e. at every point the clockwise moment must balance the anti-clockwise moment. If this were not the case then the whole system would start gyrating around some point like a wheel around an axle.

BEAMS AND BENDING

An **axial member** transfers loads that act in the same direction as the member, as in the example of potatoes on the head. A **beam** transfers loads that act in a different direction to the member – usually at right angles to the member, as in the see-saw. The loads cause moments which are resisted by the strength of the beam. The larger the moment, the stronger the beam has to be.

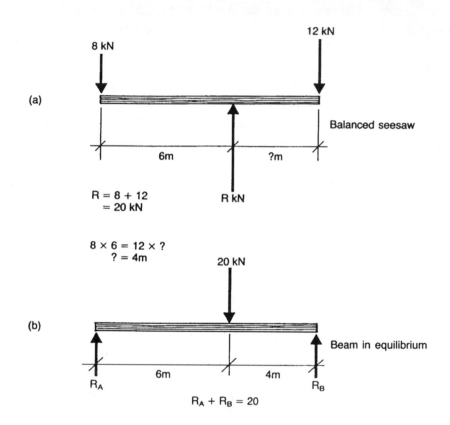

Figure 7.3 Beams and bending.

At every point on the beam, there is a moment. In Figure 7.3, the moments under the point load are:

moment to the left (anti-clockwise) = $6 \times 8 = 48$ kNm
moment to the right (clockwise) = $4 \times 12 = 48$ kNm

The turning effects are balanced and the beam has to be strong enough to generate a balancing moment of 48 kNm.

At a point 1 m from R_A:

moment to the left (anti-clockwise) $= R_A \times 1 = 8 \times 1 = 8$ kNm
moment to the right (clockwise) $= (R_A \times 9) - (20 \times 5) = (12 \times 9) - (20 \times 5) = 108 - 100 = 8$ kNm

At this point and at all the other points the moments balance. Here the beam has to be able to resist a smaller moment of 8 kNm.

The purpose of these calculations is to show how mathematics assists in structured design as well as to explain concepts. In most buildings today it is necessary to calculate loads, beam sizes, floor thicknesses and so on in order to prove that a building will stand up (e.g. for the Building Inspector) and to ensure that materials are used economically. Many of you reading this book will never have to do a calculation. However, everyone experiences structure in their daily lives and the professional needs to understand the choices available and their broad limitations.

A beam is required to resist different moments at different points along its length. What is normally of most concern is the size of the largest moment and how big the beam has to be in order to be able to produce a sufficiently large resisting moment. The size of the moment is determined by the force times the lever arm, so that the larger the load and the longer the span, the bigger the moments will be. Generally a beam of bigger span will have more load acting upon it and the maximum moment is proportional to the square of the span.

THE MAXIMUM BENDING MOMENT

Beams generate resisting moments by getting tension forces and compression forces to act against each other at a distance.

If you draw a careful picture of a beam resting on supports at each end and supporting a load in the middle, you will see that the beam will bend under the loading. When this happens the top of the beam must be getting shorter and the bottom of the beam longer. This means that the top must be in compression and generating compression forces and the bottom in tension and generating tension forces.

There is a transitional change from the top to the bottom of the beam and at some point there is a change from compression to tension. In this zone there is no force acting and so it is called the **neutral axis**. The opposing tension and compression turn about the neutral axis and create the **resisting bending moment**.

GENERATING RESISTING MOMENTS

The size of the moment is the product of the force and the length of the lever arm. The size of the force is determined by two things: the stress in the material and the area of the beam over which the stress acts. The length of the lever arm is determined by the depth of the beam.

Thus the ability of the beam to resist bending is influenced by three factors:

● the shape of the section;
● the size of the section;
● the material of which the beam is made.

In general, the deeper a beam is, the better it will resist bending. The visual proportions of most structural members are limited by practical constraints. To an experienced eye, a beam that is more than 24 times longer than it is deep will look unrealistically slender. A beam that is less than 15 times longer than it is deep will look somewhat stumpy. These crude rules of thumb are very useful when testing out alternatives at an initial design stage. They are important for not only the designer but also the client, user, other professionals and the public. The greater the understanding of the basic principles of what makes a building visually attractive – among professionals and the public – the more likely we are to create a sympathetic, attractive environment. What other considerations do we need to take into account? The following sections explore some of them.

MATERIALS

Construction textbooks of the 1960s often claimed that a bewildering number of new materials were being introduced to building. While this is true of construction in general, the materials for structures are few and well established. No new material for building structures has been introduced this century. This is because they need to have three basic characteristics: durability, cheapness and strength.

DURABILITY People have different expectations about how long particular artefacts should last. If a motor car lasts for ten years without major repair to the bodywork, the owner will be very pleased. Clothes may be thrown away after a year or two. Building structures are expected to last for a very long time and indeed only on an ancient monument would it be considered reasonable to have to replace a structure.

3

E MODEL

of a structure to perform a specific task
m high to carry a brick, or a bridge to span
a tin of paint) as efficiently as possible.
rials that have characteristic structural

properties which can be related to compression, tension
and bending (e.g. fishing line, drinking straws, paper,
card, wooden strip, drink cans).

Figure 7.4 The Pompidou Centre, Paris, designed by Richard Rogers and Partners. (Tony Collier.)

The structure is essentially the servant of the total design. It may be discrete and invisible; it may have a major role to play in how a form or a space is understood. It may make an important contribution to the reading of a particular place that reinforces the programme of the building. What clearly it should not do is to get in the way or interfere with other aspects of the building. A column in the wrong place can interrupt a sight line or interfere with a circulation flow. A deep beam above a space can divide it in a way that is alien to the way the space is intended to function. Structural members and service ducts regularly wish to occupy the same space.

CHEAPNESS   Relative to most artefacts, buildings are very large and so use up a correspondingly large quantity of material in their construction. If the basic material cost is high, then that is reflected in the cost of the building. Part of the cost of any material is the amount of money required to transport it from the point of manufacture to the site. Materials that are produced near the location of the building clearly will be relatively cheaper. A material that would perform perfectly well all the structural tasks expected of it may well be discounted simply because it is more expensive. The factors that decide the cost of a material vary considerably from one country to another. This may be due to the local availability of raw materials but is also influenced by the traditions of the building industry. As an example, two countries that are very similar in terms of economic development, France and Britain, have quite different attitudes to precast concrete. In France, for the last 50 years it has been used very widely for everything from road signs to church steeples and contemporary public housing schemes use complicated classical details cast in concrete. In Britain, precast concrete has only been used in relatively specialized circumstances and such detailed work would be prohibitively expensive. Cheapness is a product of familiarity.

STRENGTH   It goes without saying that structural materials must be reliably strong. Strength must also be associated with robustness. By using a very high strength material it might be possible to carry the loads on extremely slender structural elements. These elements would however also have to withstand loads caused by an accident or vandalism. There is a general requirement that structures should be sufficiently robust so that any one part can be removed without the whole edifice collapsing catastrophically. For instance, an out-of-control truck could remove a roadside column but the rest of the building should stay intact.

What kind of materials are used for building structures? Is there an enormous variety? How do we categorize them?

There are in fact only four materials that are regularly used for building structures and they can be divided into the traditional and the modern.

The traditional materials are **timber** and **masonry.** Masonry includes natural stone cut into blocks, clay fired into bricks, and cement and sand manufactured into blocks. For structural purposes they are all treated the same.

CHOICE OF MATERIAL

The modern materials are **steel** and **reinforced concrete**. Although they are both thought of as being modern, steel and reinforced concrete have been in use for more than 100 years. Steel is an alloy of iron and carbon and has been mass produced since the late nineteenth century. Other alloys of iron, such as cast iron and wrought iron, have been used for much longer though today they have been almost entirely replaced by steel. More modern materials such as aluminium and plastic are only used very rarely for structures.

Students often ask: 'What is the best material for my project?' It is a question to which there is no easy answer. Each material is quite different, with properties that generate different forms, as will be discussed later. Each has characteristics that may be utilized effectively in different circumstances. Many designers have strong emotive attachments to a particular material. Designers who think of themselves as being modern and technologically progressive (for example, Sir Richard Rogers or Nicholas Grimshaw) favour steel although it is hardly a contemporary material. Other designers have an affinity for timber since it comes directly from nature and can be considered to be 'green'. In Scotland, stone is thought of as the national material of the country whereas brick is an alien import. In Holland no doubt the reverse is true. The interwar modernist architects preferred reinforced concrete because it was not associated with any previous forms. Materials are like forms in that 'readings' are attributed to them. These readings may be quite separate from the properties that influence their functional use.

STRUCTURAL FORM

So far two aspects of structural design have been described:

- the forces of nature that have to be balanced in any structure that sits on the crust of the earth;
- the four materials from which building structures are conventionally made.

The task of the structural designer is to create a form from the available material that will transfer the forces of nature through the building's structure and into the ground. It is useful to think of the structure as a series of routes. These routes are the paths along which the forces pass on their way to the ground.

Once created, the structural form has to be judged or assessed from several standpoints:

- Strength – carrying loads safely
- Economy – avoiding waste
- Correspondence – relating to the overall design
- Buildability – relating to the method of construction.

The structure has to be strong enough to carry the load without disturbing the working of the building. This does not mean that it absolutely solid and immovable. When required to carry extra load beams bend a little, compression members are squashed and tension members are stretched. On conventional buildings these movements are too small to be noticed. On the very largest buildings the movement may be large and the occupants have to get used to the visible effects either directly or indirectly. In the USA there are a number of giant tower blocks containing more than 100 floors. In a high wind these buildings resist the sideways forces by swaying slowly to and fro. It is not often possible to see this movement against a fixed reference point but it is apparent enough when pendant lights and water in the wash-basins move with them. Buildings also move when they expand and contract with changes in temperature. The structure must be strong enough to carry the load and any movement must not interfere with the serviceability of the building. However, for the sake of economy, the structure should not be too strong.

Designers like to think that their designs are efficient and economic. Their clients certainly wish to be told that they are. Efficiency is an elusive quality to measure. Engineers can 'optimize' their design by ensuring that the minimum quantity of material is used, but minimum quantity is only an aspect of efficiency and is quite different from minimum cost. A light structure is often rather complicated and difficult to manufacture. It may require large amounts of energy and consume material in the process of construction for an end result that saves only a marginal amount of material. It may be time-consuming and therefore expensive to construct, which also delays the point at which other processes may begin.

The designer has to try to see the whole process and strive to ensure that at least it is not wasteful.

The structure has to have an appropriate correspondence with every other aspect of the overall architectural design.

WORKPIECE 7.

STRUCTUR

Build a model
(e.g. a tower 1
1 m and carr
Choose mat

CORRESPOND

Figure 7.5 The Lloyds Building, London, designed by Richard Rogers and Partners. (Tom Muir.)

The structure has to be appropriately integrated into the total design. That is why all students of architecture have to be taught the rudiments of structural design. They need to establish the principles of the structural form and be conscious of the routes that the forces have to follow. They should also be able to establish an effective dialogue with the specialist design engineer.

For a straightforward domestic building one person may do the whole design. For any building much bigger than that a team is required. Each member must be able to play their own part fully but must be aware of the other roles and be able to predict and accommodate how propositions will evolve and ensure that the parts make a comprehensive whole.

BUILDABILITY

The structural form should also respond to the process of constructing the building. In the normal sequence of construction, the structure goes up first and then the non-structural parts are connected to it. This means that the structural form must be compatible with the construction method. If the building has to be built very quickly, a prefabricated frame may be assembled within a few days.

ELEMENTS OF STRUCTURAL FORM

Looking at slides, books, magazines and building sites, there seems to be a bewildering range of structural possibilities. The permutations are not quite so bewildering if you remember that there are four basic ways of transferring loads (compression, tension, bending and shearing) and four common structural materials (timber, masonry, steel and reinforced concrete).

Consider also the basic architectural goal of enclosing space. This implies some kind of covering element that transfers load sideways and some kind of surrounding element connected to the ground that transfers load downwards. That is not far from saying a roof or floor is bending, carried by walls or columns in compression. This is a very simple view but it applies to a lot of buildings.

WORKPIECE 7.4

PUBLIC BUILDINGS

Choose a large public building (e.g. a town hall, sports hall, railway station). Look at it carefully from the outside and choose a large space inside.

Note carefully every part of the building that you can see that tells you anything about the structure of the building – columns, walls, arches, beams, trusses, ribs, lintels, struts, ties etc. Also note anything that appears to be enclosing or covering up a piece of structure.

Draw an exterior and an interior diagram of what you have noted and what it tells you about the whole structural arrangement.

Write down what messages the structure suggests to you. For example:

- Does it suggest balance or equilibrium?
- Does it suggest harmony and order?
- Does it suggest solidity or fragility?
- Does it suggest efficiency and economy?
- Does it suggest drama and daring?

What else does it suggest?

MATERIALS AND FORM

What is the relationship between structures, materials and forms? Do some materials lend themselves to particular kinds of building and style? How can we recognize the type of structure that holds up a building by looking at the facade?

Some structural materials naturally produce a particular range of forms; others are extremely flexible and have no obvious preferred form. We shall now consider the common materials and place them in an approximate range of forms. This way round is in the end more straightforward than listing forms and relating them to materials.

All types of masonry can be made into three basic forms:

- A vertical surface made of overlapping blocks that is very strong in compression but very weak in tension or bending. The strength depends as much on the mortar which glues the block together as on the strength of the blocks themselves.
- Arrangement in separate piers or columns, where the width and depth are much less than the height.
- Curved surfaces of masonry. Before the arrival of steel and reinforced concrete, these were used in the form of compression arches to transfer loads sideways.

Basically all forms of masonry transfer loads by compression systems. While it is possible to have hybrid systems that act as bending elements, this can only be done where another material (normally steel) is used to take the tension. An example of this would be reinforced brickwork.

You may have noticed that in this chapter words like 'normally' and usually' are used regularly. This is because it is important for students to appreciate the contrast between a method which is used everyday and in nearly all buildings and a method which is quite practical and interesting but is only very rarely used, perhaps in rather special circumstances.

Compression structures in masonry are a good example of this distinction:

- Masonry walls are the most common building element. They are found in one form or another in almost every building.
- Masonry columns or piers are unusual but you would not be surprised to find them in a new building.
- Masonry arches are extremely rare in a new building of the second half of the twentieth century. Although it was a commonplace method in previous centuries, it is hard to think of a single modern example of a genuine masonry arch. There are plenty of examples of brick or stone arches being attached to a steel or reinforced concrete structure but none of them are actually used to carry load – they are simply decorative.

Bricks and blocks come in standard sizes. In order to construct a wall they are placed in an overlapping pattern called bonding. The joints between them are filled with mortar made from a mixture of sand, cement and sometimes lime.

In building, a masonry wall has many uses in addition to carrying load. Generally the non-structural task of the wall is of greater importance than the structural one. In most cases, therefore, the wall is much thicker and stronger than it would need to be just to carry the load. Many walls are simply used to define space and carry no load except their own weight. These are called non-loadbearing walls.

Once you make an opening in a wall for a window or a door or any other reason, the load above the opening has to be carried sideways. In previous centuries an arch would often have been used but today it is always a horizontal bending member called a **lintel**. These beams can be either steel or reinforced concrete. Different kinds of opening have been used extensively in different periods by different civilizations. The functions of the openings are relatively limited. Their style and appearance can vary enormously but this is more to do with visual issues than structure. There are only a limited number of ways that an opening can be made in a wall structurally.

Walls form the boundaries of spaces. When openings are made the space changes. When a wall stops the space changes, but while the wall surface is present it exerts a powerful and particular architectural influence. If the compression loads are brought down through columns located at separate points perhaps 7 m apart, then the influence on the space is quite different.

TIMBER

Structural timber is now cut from the trunks of coniferous trees. This is transformed into two types of element: 'sticks' and sheets.

'STICKS'   Rectangular solid sections may be up to 6 m long but are rarely more than 300 mm thick. Think of them as sticks. They come directly from the tree and have the benefits and drawbacks of a natural material. They are composed of hollow fibres that run longitudinally up and down the tree's trunk carrying nutrients to feed its growth. Like a bundle of tubes, they are much stronger in the long direction than they are in the cross direction. These timber 'sticks' are usually assembled into an open framework which carries the load. It uses the infilling material to give it continuity strength. The linear sections are very good at carrying axial tension and compression load. They also work very well in bending to make very useful beams. In the past very large trees (hardwoods such as oak) were available and massive sections were used but today smaller softwood trees are used and timber as a structural material is limited by the sizes of the sections that are available.

SHEETS   Trunks are converted into sheets (such as plywood, chipboard and blockboard) usually 2.4 m by 1.2 m and between 10 mm and 20 mm thick. They are rarely used on their own but in conjunction with a solid section to give continuity and to aid jointing.

JOINTING   There is a tradition in Japan that elevates the jointing of timber to a mystic art. In the West modern technology such as synthetic glues and steel connectors have made the process more straightforward but the joint is still one of the most challenging aspects of designing in timber.

STEEL

Steel is produced in huge sophisticated industrial plants in developed countries all over the world. Only a small proportion of their output is structural steel for use in building structures. Relative to the other three materials, structural steel is very strong and very expensive.

In other respects as a general building material steel performs rather badly. If exposed to air and water, it rusts; if heated to above 550°C, it loses all its strength. Steel structures therefore have to be designed to use the minimum amount of material and to be carefully protected.

The steel plants produce standard linear sections which are assembled into frameworks connected by welding or bolting. These frameworks form an armature which can be erected quickly. Afterwards all the other elements of the enclosure can be attached to it. Generally these frameworks are rectilinear assemblies with the occasional diagonal member for bracing. In recent years extraordinary machines have been developed which can take a steel section perhaps 800 mm by 400 mm and bend it into a radius. This technical innovation has enabled the curved steel beam to become the icon of the late 20th century postmodern style.

In a similar way the icon of the 'high tech' style is the steel tension cable. Steel is in reality the only material that is suitable for pure tension members. The detailed technology for analysing and connecting steel cables was worked out in the construction of long-span bridges and then transferred for use in building. As structures get larger, it becomes progressively more important that the structure material carries the maximum amount of load using the least amount of weight. It is for this reason that all the very tall buildings, such as the American skyscrapers that are more than 100 storeys high are carried by steel frames. Similarly all the really long-span roof structures are made from steel frame lattice stuctures.

WORKPIECE 7.5

ROOF SUPPORTS

Go to your local railway station or football stadium. Draw as accurately as you can on an A1 sheet of paper the principal structural member supporting the roof. This will commonly be a steel lattice truss and you must be careful to get the correct geometry of the members and consider carefully how the members are jointed together.

REINFORCED CONCRETE   In many respects reinforced concrete is the complete opposite of structural steel. It is cheap, easy to make, durable, fireproof and extremely versatile. In terms of the ratio between the amount of load carried and self-weight, however, it is not nearly as strong.

Its appearance reflects the manner in which it is produced. Any DIY enthusiast can knock together some gravel, sand, cement and water, reinforce it with some steel wire and produce a garden wall or a front driveway. The process of construction will be clearly seen in the lack of smoothness of finish, the joints and the variation in colour etc. In contrast a welded steel frame can give the appearance of a machine-made artefact without blemish or indication of how it came about.

Reinforced concrete offers cheap mass which is very necessary for foundations, floors and other elements of a building that for functional reasons need to be 'solid'.

SUMMARY

A building, like every other object that sits on the earth's crust, has to have a structure that can carry loads and transfer them into the ground. Structures work by deforming in one of four ways and are usually made from one of four materials.

A structural design of quality does its own job efficiently and contributes positively to the total architectural design.

KEY CONCEPTS

- Only in this century have designers needed to describe their structures in numerical terms.
- All gravity forces have in the end to be absorbed into the crust of the earth. There are four basic mechanisms for transferring forces: compression, tension, bending and shear.
- Forces in all directions must balance.
- Structural materials need to be durable, cheap and strong.

- There are four basic materials used for building structures: masonry and timber (traditional), steel and reinforced concrete (modern).
- The task of the structural designer is to create a form from the available materials that will transfer the forces of nature through the building and into the ground.
- The structure should have an appropriate correspondence with every other aspect of the overall architectural design.
- The basic materials have properties that tend to generate particular forms.

FURTHER READING

Benjamin, B.S. (1984) *Structures for Architects*, Nostrand-Rheinhold.

Cowan, H.J. (1977) *The Master Builders*, Wiley.

Cowan, H.J. and Wilson, F. (1981) *Structural Systems*, Nostrand-Rheinhold.

Gauld, B.J.B. (1988) *Structures for Architects*, Longmans.

Gordon, J.E. (1978) *Structures, or why things don't fall down*, Penguin.

Hodgkinson, A. (1980) *AJ Handbook of Building Structures*, Architectural Press.

Holgate, A. (1986) *The Art in Structural Design*, Clarendon.

Mainstone, R.J. (1975) *Developments in Structural Form*, RIBA Publications.

Salvadori, M. (1980) *Why Buildings Stand Up: the strength of architecture*, Rheinhold.

Sandaker, N.S and Eggen, A.P. (1992) *The Structural Basis of Architecture*, Whitney Library of Design.

CHAPTER EIGHT

THE BUILDING SKIN

ROBERT GRIMSHAW AND ARTHUR YARNELL

THEME

The key determinant in modifying climate is the nature of the building 'skin'. Whether this is traditional brickwork or a modern glass construction, it is primarily the 'skin' of the building that ensures appropriate modification of the physical conditions between the inside and outside of a building. There are many existing and contrasting examples of building skins. Some are integral to the structure of the building (for example, an igloo), others have no structural significance other than supporting themselves (for example, glass curtain walling). A mud and thatch house in the Amazon basin has no skin apart from the roof and low walls, yet it modifies climate.

OBJECTIVES

At the end of this chapter you should be able to:

● understand the principles of modifying the environment by means of the skin of a building;

● identify how different materials and construction techniques are used to modify climate.

INTRODUCTION

What lessons can be learnt from simple shelters about the importance of the building skin?

Many cities around the world are surrounded by shanty towns consisting of a variety of the most primitive buildings. In Chapter 2 we discussed the movements of people and the need to create even the most basic structures from the point of view of solid walls. But how do simple shelters perform? In this chapter we will investigate the performance of

156

Figure 8.1 Cheap and available materials used to create a simple dwelling. (Tom Muir.)

buildings and their skin even in the most rudimentary form. Simple shelters can be made from any surplus materials that are available – corrugated iron, plastic sheeting, bits of timber, mud and straw etc. These buildings do not have even the simplest of services; there is no running water and no drainage and the living conditions are often appalling. Yet even they illustrate the importance of the building fabric or skin. The inside of a shanty is private, shielding the residents from the gaze of others; it also denotes that the family within has its own territory from which it can exclude others.

Most importantly, the skin forms a primitive but effective barrier against the worst extremes of the external climate. It provides a filtering which modifies the climate sufficiently for the internal conditions to be more acceptable. It excludes the wind and rain, keeping the inhabitants dry; it reflects and absorbs the sun's rays during the day, providing shade, and with a simple fire inside it helps to limit the worst of the cold at night. In short, the external fabric or skin of a building allows the inhabitants to filter the external environment and to provide an enclosed space so that human activities can take place in a regulated environment.

THE BUILDING SKIN

Although the skins of modern buildings are much more sophisticated than those of a shanty, much of the same purpose is served. The majority of human activities take place in buildings and part of the function of the building is to ensure that the internal conditions are right for that activity to take place. As well as maintaining a regulated enclosed space, the external fabric of a building has other important functions to perform.

- It has an important part to play in the structural stability of the building.
- It gives the building its aesthetic qualities and determines its visual characteristics of expression.
- It allows direct and indirect contact between the outside world and the interior of the building in an acceptable form.

This chapter is mainly concerned with the way in which the skin of the building filters the external climate to provide acceptable internal conditions. However, the other functions of the skin have to be taken into account in its design and it is the main purpose of a designer to achieve a reasonable balance between all these functional requirements. To take an extreme example, it would be possible to build a structure with no windows and very thick, highly insulated walls where the loss of heat through the structure was very low, making it very energy efficient; however, the lack of windows and any contact with the outside world are likely to make it psychologically unacceptable. Similarly, a glass box would allow almost unrestricted visual contact between the inside and outside of a building but would not permit internal privacy and is likely to have very high levels of heat loss. So the design of the external fabric of a building is a complex process comprising the selection of appropriate materials and construction techniques to balance the competing functional requirements, of which climate modification is one major factor.

WORKPIECE 8.1

FUNCTIONAL REQUIREMENTS OF THE SKIN

List the essential functions or performance characteristics which the skins of dwelling house should possess.

Compare and prioritize these requirements in the following situations:

- Low-cost housing in Africa.
- Housing provided by the State in Russia.
- Private dwellings in France.

The skin is the whole envelope of the building, including the walls and roof, and is a mixture of different building materials which are assembled together into building elements to make up the structures which form the skin. A typical domestic dwelling in the UK, for example, might have walls which contain clay bricks, concrete blocks, sand-and-cement mortar, plastic damp-courses, galvanized steel lintels, non-ferrous wall ties, mineral fibre insulation material, and gypsum plaster. It would also incorporate other prefabricated components, such as doors and windows which may be constructed from wood and glass. Each of these materials has its own physical properties which, combined with the way they are assembled, determines how that part of the skin will modify the internal climate of the building in reaction to the external climate.

What are the relationships between the elements and materials? How do they interact?

The human biological system is very adaptable and enables humans to tolerate a wide range of climatic conditions. In response to high temperatures, sweat is produced to provide a cooling effect. Hair provides some protection from direct sunlight as well as a large surface area from which sweat can evaporate. People of warmer regions tend to have darker skin, a possible protection against damage from direct sun. In Arctic regions, stocky body build and generally large body size are more common, and these traits apparently help in conserving body heat. Light-coloured skin may be less susceptible than dark skin to frostbite. Narrow noses serve better than broad noses to warm frigid air before it enters the lungs. All these advantageous traits are more common in northern peoples such as the Inuit (Eskimo), Lapps and Siberians. Nevertheless, basic physiological responses to cold (shivering, for instance) occur in the same way in all human groups and the most significant human adaptations to climate – clothes, dwellings and the use of fire – are cultural, not biological.

Although humans are able to survive and prosper in a range of conditions, there is only a narrow band which can be described as comfortable. It is the prime purpose of buildings to provide a way of moderating the environmental conditions so that comfort is achieved. However, defining ideal comfort conditions is difficult because of this adaptability of the human biological functioning: people become acclimatized to temperatures to which they are regularly exposed. One group of office workers in the UK described temperatures of around 22°C as comfort-

PASSIVE MODIFICATION OF THE CLIMATE

able, while similar workers in tropical countries were equally comfortable at 32°C.[1]

There are two ways of controlling the internal climate of a building to make it acceptable for the use involved. The skin of the building acts as a passive modifier or filter to the external climate. That is, the nature of the materials and the way they are put together determines the way the external climate impacts on the internal conditions.[2] However, in some climates this is not enough to ensure an acceptable internal environment at all times and active measures in the form of mechanical and non-mechanical devices have to be used to regulate the conditions. Active modifiers will be considered in Chapter 9, but it should be noted at this stage that the successful control of the internal environment is usually a combination of the passive effect of the building skin and active mechanical measures.

WORKPIECE 8.2

PASSIVE MEASURES

Suggest three reasons why society may favour a greater reliance on passive controls to form a stable internal environment rather than by the use of active systems.

When considering the concept of thermal inertia, under what circumstances is it likely to be more appropriate to adopt 'lightweight' or 'heavyweight' building forms?

The balance between the two is often determined by overall form of the building, especially in relation to heat control. A building composed of brick or concrete (i.e. heavyweight) will respond more slowly to the influences of heat than a building constructed with a timber frame (i.e. lightweight). These buildings are said to have differing thermal inertia. The former may have a very stable internal climate where passive measures predominate, whereas the latter will respond rapidly to active systems. Similarly a steel framed building where the structural action is dealt with by the overall frame may have a lightweight skin which has only a limited ability to modify the external climate, whereas a building with a loadbearing skin, where the weight of the structure is carried by the outer skin, may have a much greater scope for passive control and less need for active measures.

The building skin is therefore a composite structure of different materials where the characteristics of each material and the way they are put together determines the performance of the skin. To extend our example of the construction of a UK domestic dwelling, the materials are assembled in a cavity construction with an outer skin of bricks, a cavity containing a layer of thermal insulation and an inner skin of blockwork, the two skins being held together by metal wall ties built into the mortar joints of each skin. This form of construction is peculiar to the UK and has developed as a direct result of the climate of the UK, with its wide variations of temperature and its high rainfall.

Before we can look at how typical examples of the skin do their work, we must examine briefly what elements of the external climate are being modified and what is an acceptable internal climate.

What are the variations in global climate? How do they effect buildings?

Humans inhabit all areas of the globe, from the hottest, driest deserts to the coldest places imaginable. There are therefore wide variations in the climatic conditions which buildings must tackle and it is hardly surprising that built form varies widely to meet these conditions. Some climates are very stable (the temperature in the tropics may vary by only 5°C throughout the year) but some climates are very unstable. The temperature in a maritime climate may vary by as much as 10°C in a matter of hours, and deserts which may be baking hot during the day may be extremely cold at night. Some climates are always dry and some are always wet, while some are dry in summer and wet in winter (Tables 8.1 and 8.2).

ELEMENTS OF EXTERNAL CLIMATE

Table 8.1 Climatic temperature zones

Scale No.	Climatic zone	Period (months)	Temperature range	Temperature for the remaining period
1	Tropical	12	>20°C	
2	Subtropical	4–12	>20°C	10–20°C
3	Temperate	4–12	10–20°C	<10°C
4	Cold	1–4	10–20°C	<10°C
5	Polar	12	<10°C	

As well as temperature classification, climatologists classify zones in terms of precipitation as shown by Table 8.2. Within each hemisphere, eight basic climatological zones can also be recognized in terms of precipitation.

Table 8.2 Precipitation classifications

Scale no.	Zone	Description
1	Equatorial	Rain in all seasons
2	Tropical	Summer rain, dry winters
3	Semi-arid tropical	Slight summer rain
4	Arid	Dry in all seasons
5	Dry Mediterranean	Slight winter rain
6	Mediterranean	Winter rain summer dry
7	Temperate	Precipitation in all seasons
8	Polar	Sparse in all seasons

These variations offer different challenges to the designers of buildings and have particular relevance when considering the buildings' skin. It is difficult to make generalizations but we can make some statements about the elements of the climate that have the most effect on the interior of a building.

WORKPIECE 8.3

EXTERNAL CLIMATE

Prepare a sketch which illustrates the changing requirements of the skin of a building when it is moved from:

- a tropical climate to temperate conditions;
- a temperate environment to a polar situation;
- a polar climate to a tropical zone.

TEMPERATURE VARIATIONS

The effects of the variations in outside temperature are perhaps the most noticeable effects of the external climate on the interior of a building. There are three categories which must be considered: **tropical** (hot all the time), **polar** (cold all the time) and **temperate** (variations in hot and cold). In the tropical category the skin of the building must resist the passage of heat, reflecting as much as possible, to create cool conditions inside and counteract excessive solar gain. In the polar category, the skin must resist cold penetration and prevent as much loss of heat through the skin as possible. The temperate category can be the most difficult in design terms as it must try to do both; that is, counteract the effect of constant changes in temperature which may have a detrimental effect on the materials involved.

The presence of unnecessary water in a building may not have the immediate impact on the inhabitants as do excesses of heat or cold, but in the long term excessive moisture can have a severe effect on both the fabric of a building and its inhabitants. Water may be derived from rain, snow, frost, groundwater, humidity or condensation, all of which must be controlled by the skin. Rain and snow have greatest impact on the roof structure whereas excessive humidity will effect the whole skin. In wet climates, getting water away from the structure as soon as possible is vital. In cold climates, shedding snow quickly and efficiently is important to reduce the applied loads. In humid climates, the whole skin must be able to resist the penetration of water vapour and allow water vapour generated inside the building to escape.[3]

MOISTURE

The rate of airflow can exacerbate the effects of both temperature and moisture, and its effect is greater the more exposed the location is. Tall buildings in exposed areas may be severely affected by wind and the skin must be designed to take this into account.

AIRFLOW

How do we judge the success of the external fabric in modifying the climate? It is done by examination of how closely the internal environment matches the ideals set out at the design stage. The assessment can apply equally if the internal conditions are achieved by purely passive measures or by a mixture of both active and passive methods. It is usual at the design stage to consider the activities which are going to take place inside the building so that appropriate standards are set for the internal conditions. As the ideal internal environment varies with the activity being undertaken, it is difficult to stipulate precise comfort conditions but the following general statements can be made.

ELEMENTS OF THE INTERNAL CLIMATE

WORKPIECE 8.4

INTERNAL FACTORS

Describe what would happen to the internal climate of a modern office building in Birmingham if there was a power strike and all electric services were off.

How adequate would the skin of the building be for controlling the internal climate?

Could the building continue to be used?

Achieving thermal comfort involves controlling several factors including the air temperature, its moisture content, the temperature of surrounding surfaces and the rate of air flowing in the space. Although the mode

TEMPERATURE

of heating (conduction, convection or radiation) affects the perception of temperature, it is generally accepted that a temperature of between 18 and 22°C should be maintained for most sedentary activities in temperate climates.

AIR QUALITY

The quality of the air is affected by many factors including the extent to which external pollutants pass into the building, the number of people in the enclosed space, the type of activities being undertaken, the nature of fabrics and furnishing, the nature of waste products produced from the activities and the rate of air replacement (i.e the number of air changes per hour). External pollutants should be excluded as far as possible and where they are excessive this may mean the skin should act as a total barrier between interior and exterior. Levels of external pollutants in large conurbations, like Los Angeles and Athens, where the effect of sunlight on car exhaust emissions creates smog, already pose a danger to health and require a building where the skin seals off the outside climate. Air which is either too dry or too moist is detrimental to human activity. In a building, the oxygen can become depleted and the carbon dioxide can rise to unacceptable levels if the air is not replenished from outside. Ventilation is therefore important and serious consideration must be given to controlling the amount of external pollutants which may be passed into the building. Natural ventilation is by far the most efficient but modern buildings turn increasingly to artificial methods of restoring the quality of internal air through air-conditioning plants.[1]

LIGHTING

The sun provides a good source of natural light, and even in overcast conditions adequate lighting levels can be achieved in most buildings by appropriate design and positioning of windows. The penalty paid for this natural light is the excessive glare and thermal discomfort that can be experienced. Unlike other elements of climate, certain aspects of the sun can be accurately predicted; for example, the direction from which the sun shines is governed by time of year, time of day and geographical location. Therefore the extent to which sunlight can penetrate a room can be accurately assessed. Less predictable is the amount of time the sky is clear and direct sunlight is available. The other effect of sun is in heating of materials and components, which when exposed to direct sunlight expand and contract so that, where different materials are used, differential movements are possible. Notwithstanding these limitations good daylighting is considered too important to people's physiological well-being in buildings. Although artificial lighting is more than adequate for people to see, it does have a detrimental effect if used exclusively. It is important, therefore, that the skin of the building admits sufficient daylight.[2]

DEVELOPMENT OF THE BUILDING SKIN

In looking at the way that building skins have developed over time, the four criteria which were introduced at the beginning of this chapter (structural action, aesthetic quality, link between inside and outside, as well as the degree of passive filtering or environmental control) must be remembered. It is important to consider these aspects of the skin because the relationship between such criteria has altered as technology has changed over the last 2000 years.

Two distinct patterns have affected the development of the building skin. The first is a switch from a situation where largely local materials were used except for high prestige buildings, to one where there is an international market in building materials and therefore much more standardization of materials and components.[4] The second is a move from buildings where the passive measures of climate control predominated, largely because of a lack of mechanical active devices, to one where active devices and the means of controlling them are proliferating and less importance is being placed on passive measures of control. We shall look first at vernacular building techniques to assess the use of local materials and then consider the wider movements in Western architecture to look at the impact of technological changes.

WORKPIECE 8.5

DEVELOPMENT

Over the last 200 years the building skin has evolved to become a highly sophisticated element of construction. Consider what has contributed to this rapid rate of change and suggest what technological developments might lead to further development over the next 100 years.

SMALL-SCALE BUILDINGS

Vernacular architecture means the use of local materials and styles, giving distinct variations in built form and the materials used across the globe. We shall consider this first on a world-wide basis and then look at its impact on the UK.

Geographical localities can either have a very rich variety of building materials or, at the other extreme, complete lack of local materials. In SE Asia the use of bamboo, a very light but very strong form of timber which is able to resist tensile forces, has made it easy for local people to build large sophisticated dwellings using bamboo as a basis, supplemented by the use of dried grasses for roofing material. In contrast, Eskimos have an almost total lack of any building materials in their Arctic homeland but use what is available – blocks of ice – to build an adequate shelter which exploits the insulating effect of snow (the form of the igloo in a hemisphere is forced by the physical properties of the ice and its inability to resist tensile forces). American Indians had material available to construct substantial permanent dwellings, as shown by the ruins of the stone pueblos of the Anasazi Indians, but the nomadic life of some tribes as they followed the buffalo herds meant a portable dwelling was essential and the Indian tepee made simply from timber poles and buffalo hide proved an effective answer. The ability of the skin to resist the external climate was minimal but had to be sacrificed for portability.[4]

WORKPIECE 8.6

SHELTER

Make a drawing of a shelter you have designed using only straws 1 m long and rubber bands.
How effective a shelter do you think it would be?

Even a geographically small country like the UK displays a wide range of vernacular styles. Until the Industrial Revolution stone, which was an expensive material both to quarry and transport, was used only for prestige buildings apart from areas where it was readily obtainable. In the Pennine uplands, longhouses (a combination of house and barn) were constructed with stone walls and slate on the roof, because stone was plentiful and timber scarce. However, in most lowland areas, timber was available and used for the structure of dwellings from the Dark Ages to the Industrial Revolution. Regional variations were expressed in the filling between the timber frame: for example, in Kent, where timber was plentiful, timber and weather boarding was the norm; in parts of the Midlands, where clay was available, brick infill was used; in Norfolk, with neither brick nor timber in plentiful supply, flints were used and set in a lime mortar. Roofing showed similar variations. In clay areas, clay tiles similar to those used by the Romans were used. In Norfolk, reeds were popular for thatch; whilst in the north, stone slates were employed.

Thus early building forms were crude and based on local materials. Dwellings were cold and draughty and lacked internal services apart from a fire. Vernacular architecture diminished in importance after the Industrial Revolution in the nineteenth century. The growth of mass manufacture of building materials, and the ability to transport heavy goods cheaply and quickly by rail, led to an increasingly homogeneous building style and form.[4, 5]

Until the Industrial Revolution there were relatively few non-domestic dwellings (apart from large gathering centres) but since the mid nineteenth century the growth of the commercial, industrial and public sectors has produced large quantities of non-domestic building.

LARGE-SCALE BUILDING

During the early phases of Western architecture from the Roman period to the early Middle Ages, the needs of the structure predominated and consequently walls were thick and pierced by few windows. The Pantheon in Rome (Chapter 6) is a good example.[4] The structural action of the dome can only be accommodated by the massive structure of the stone walls, leaving little scope for the walls to allow daylight through. Even though the walls have a high thermal inertia and provide a very even temperature inside, it is purely a by-product of their massiveness – there was no other way to achieve the architectural and structural performance. Compare this with the York Minster, a Gothic cathedral built in the Middle Ages. Even though the building material is the same, the use of vaulting and flying buttresses to deal with the structural actions means a much lighter skin is achieved, allowing large areas of windows to be included and a much closer relationship between the interior and exterior of the building. In this period most prestige buildings were of stone with pitched slated or leaded roofs. The materials used in the building skin could only resist compressive forces and so tensile loads had to be avoided.

It was only with the Industrial Revolution that materials started to be produced which would resist tensile forces. This allowed a much greater freedom in the way the skin of a building could be designed, particularly the use of cast iron, wrought iron and then steel. The Crystal Palace, a building which changed the way people perceived large structures, was a totally glazed prefabricated building which was dismantled and moved from Hyde Park to Beckenham in south London when the 1851 Great Exhibition was completed; it survived until 1936. The characteristics of the skin were very different from the heavyweight buildings of the time and produced the internal effect of lightness that the name suggests. The use of iron beams at railway termini like St Pancras allowed huge spans to be achieved across the trains sheds whilst allowing light into the interior in a way still admired today. In general, however, walls and roofs remained traditional in form but used the more widely available materials of brick and slate, as well as stone and tiles.

The combination of steel framing, freeing the skin from its load-bearing function, and the development of electric lifts allowed the development of the first buildings to rise above six storeys in the last decade of the nineteenth century. This, along with the development of reinforced concrete, led to the high-rise buildings that have character-ized the twentieth century. This development has been accompanied by the growth of active building services (as discussed in detail in Chapter 9) to the point where today a totally sealed building with an internally generated environment is possible. The skin of these buildings is freed from its structural function and its function as an environmental filter is lessened.[6] Figure 8.2 shows a section through the skin of a typical glazed high rise building where the skin has little structural function.

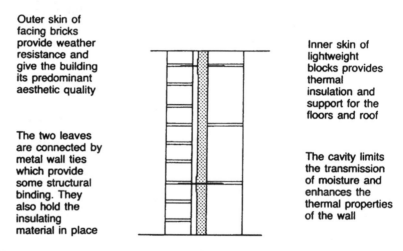

Outer skin of facing bricks provide weather resistance and give the building its predominant aesthetic quality

Inner skin of lightweight blocks provides thermal insulation and support for the floors and roof

The two leaves are connected by metal wall ties which provide some structural binding. They also hold the insulating material in place

The cavity limits the transmission of moisture and enhances the thermal properties of the wall

Figure 8.2   Cross-section through a cavity wall

Excessive solar gain in glazed buildings has made designers aware of unintended environmental effects and design measures are now com-mon in terms of reflective glass and sun shades. Perhaps the ultimate building skin is that of the Arab Centre in Paris which reacts to sunlight and automatically adjusts to allow a set amount of heat and light through it, a move from passive filtering to active control by the skin similar to that of the human body.

The number of ways in which the skin of a building can be con-structed is manifold: however, Figures 8.2 and 8.3, showing a section through a cavity wall typical of UK domestic construction and a section through a glass curtain wall of a typical modern commercial building, will give some idea of how building skins are constructed and how the combination of materials can filter the external climate and modify the internal climate.

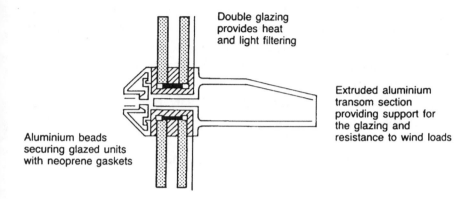

Figure 8.3 Cross-section through a curtain wall.

SUMMARY

This chapter has looked at how the skin of a building modifies and filters the elements of the external climate to make the internal climate of the building more suitable for human use; this applies from the most primitive shelter to the most sophisticated modern building. The ability of the skin to make modifications is passive and relies on the physical characteristics of the materials involved and the way they are put together. However, the building skin has several functions including structural action and aesthetic qualities: these may conflict with its role as a climatic filter and the design team has to balance out these conflicting needs to produce an acceptable solution.

The type of skin adopted for any particular building is determined by two things: firstly, the external climate in terms of temperature, moisture, rainfall, wind and the degree of exposure of the building; secondly, by the internal requirements of the building users. This has led to a wide variety of building skin types being developed both geographically and over time. Vernacular buildings have relied on locally available materials, leading to buildings as diverse as igloos and tepees. Even in a country as small as the UK there was a large variety of vernacular types of walling and roofing to infill the basic timber frame of a building: in many places only prestige buildings like cathedrals, churches and the houses of the aristocracy were built in stone. However, the industrial revolution and the development of mass production of building material and cheap transport have lead to the adaptation of national and universal styles of building skin and the local variations have largely been lost.

Technical developments, especially the increase in active services in the twentieth century and the development of steel and concrete frames, have freed the skin from its structural functions with developments like curtain walling which have also reduced its need to act as a climatic modifier. However, perhaps these innovations have not been completely successful and many will welcome the return to the more traditional forms of building skin, especially brickwork and pitched roofs, of the post-modernist age.

KEY CONCEPTS

- The building skin modifies the external environment to make the interior more acceptable.
- The ability of the skin to modify the climate is dependent on physical form of the materials and the way they are put together.
- The building skin has more than one function.
- The skin must react to the external climate.
- The skin must respond to the internal requirements.
- The skins of many buildings world-wide are influenced by the availability of local materials, with only prestige building using expensive materials like stone.
- The evolution of the building skin has been influenced by developments in technology and transport since the industrial revolution.
- The development of active building services has lessened the modifying nature of the building skin.

REFERENCES

1. Microsoft Corporation (1993) *Climate, in Encarta*, Funk & Wagnall's Corporation.
2. Osbourn, D. (1993) *Introduction to Buildings* (Mitchells Building Series), Longman.
3. Foster, S. (1993) *Structure of Fabric* (Mitchells Building Series), Longman.
4. Mainstone, R.J. (1983) *Developments in Structural Form*, Penguin.
5. Balcombe, G. (1985) *History of Building* (Mitchells Building Series), Longman.
6. Brookes, A.J. (1990) *Claddings of Buildings*, Longman.

Balcombe, G. (1985) *History of Building Styles, Methods and Materials*, Batsford Academic & Educational, London.

Barry, R. (1989) *The Construction of Buildings 1*, 5th edn, BSP Professional Books.

Brooks, A.J. and Grech, C. (1993) *The Building Envelope*, Butterworth.

Chudley, R. (1988) *Building Construction Handbook*, Heinemann Newnes.

Fielden, B.M. (1994) *Conservation of Historic Buildings*, Butterworth Scientific.

Foster, S. (1994) *Mitchell's Structure and Fabric, Part 1*, 5th edn, Longman Scientific & Technical.

Hinks, A. and Cook, G.K. (1992) *Appraising Building Defects*, Longman.

Reid, E. (1984) *Understanding Buildings – A multidisciplinary approach*, Longman Scientific & Technical.

Taylor, G.D. and Smith, B.J. *Materials in Construction*, Longman.

ASPECTS OF ENGINEERING SERVICES IN DESIGN AND DEVELOPMENT

ROBERT GRIMSHAW AND ROBERT TEMPLETON

THEME

Services and services engineering are an increasingly important part of any building project. One of the earliest known forms of ducted warm air was in Roman villas. The evolution of services from basic plumbing to 'high tech' buildings today has great significance for all aspects of the development process. The relationship between the servicing needs of individual buildings and infrastructure requirements is touched on.

OBJECTIVES

At the end of this chapter you should be able to:

- appreciate that building services have evolved;

- appreciate the breadth of services engineering skills involved in the built environment;

- understand the interrelationship between the design and installation of services and the overall building design;

- assess the roles of services and their contribution to a 'quality environment'.

The incorporation of engineering services within buildings has to do with the provision of a safe, comfortable and convenient environment: safety in the form of fire and security detection systems and fire fighting installations; comfort in the form of heating and air-conditioning systems and convenience in systems such as lighting installations, lifts and communications systems.

It is evident that from the earliest times humans have sought to modify their living conditions, not only by the use of built structures but by servicing them. The earliest examples of services in buildings include heating by open fires and the provision of water.

Since the Industrial Revolution we have had both the technology and the wealth to develop ever more sophisticated services systems.

The development of building services in Western architecture has not been linear. The Romans developed effective non-mechanical systems to service buildings which were not surpassed in Western Europe until the Industrial Revolution. A typical Roman villa might have had underfloor central heating with warm flue gases being circulated under floors and through wall flues to radiate heat into rooms. It might have had running water delivered to the dwelling in lead pipes and a drainage system to take away waste water and human waste products. Heated baths were also commonly provided.

With the demise of the Roman Empire in Western Europe this technology was largely lost and services systems were in the main confined to open fire heating. Drainage was non-existent and there are many stories of the rubbish and human waste in the streets of mediaeval towns.[1] Such poor provision for sanitation led to frequent outbreaks of diseases like cholera and the plague.

Even as late as the eighteenth century, a typical dwelling in the UK would only have heating by open fires, lighting by candle, no sanitation and an external source of water supply.

The Industrial Revolution, however, produced both the wealth and the technology necessary to ensure the rapid growth of building services, which has continued to the present.

The first works in the nineteenth century (for example, the provision of public utilities such as water supplies and sewage systems) were motivated by the desire to rid industrial cities of cholera. Other developments of the infrastructure such as gas and electrical supplies have allowed the development of our modern services installations and the demand for these has in turn increased the demand for the provision of utilities.

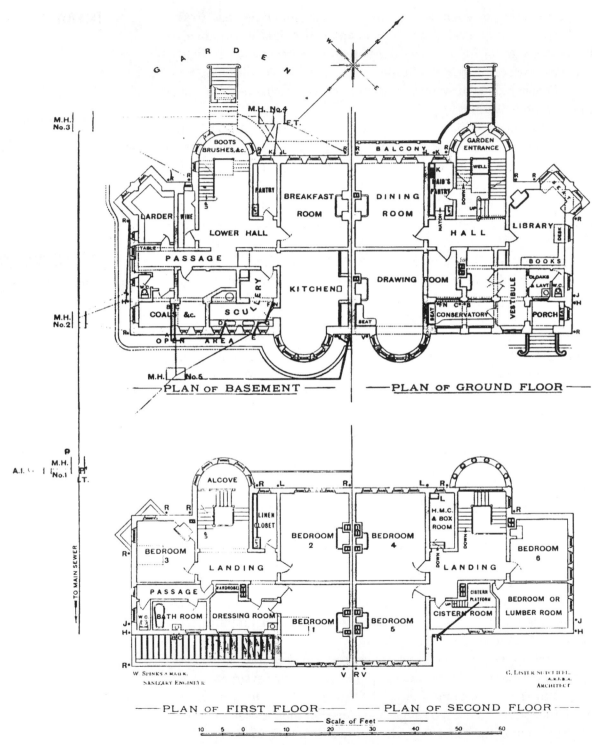

Figure 9.1 Plans showing sanitary fittings and drainage of a pair of suburban houses, *ca.* 1900.

Water power started the Industrial Revolution, turning factory machinery. This was soon superseded by steam power, fuelled by coal, but still initially being used to drive machinery in individual factories or to drive canal or mining pumps.

In the late nineteenth century gas was the first fuel to be piped from a central plant to individual buildings, providing lighting. The gas was distributed within the buildings through a pipework system to individual gas mantles. However, it was the distribution of electrical power to individual buildings which made possible the rapid development of the services systems that we currently enjoy. It is the key to improvement in the quality and sophistication of building services.

Most services systems rely upon electrical power. Indeed many of them have been developed on the basis of its availability. Early hot-water central heating systems were driven by convection but the introduction of the electrically powered pump resulted in greatly increased circulation pressures, allowing a spectacular reduction in pipe sizes (from 75 mm down to 12 mm) and the incorporation of complex control systems.

Power networks are, however, only part of a wider services infrastructure on which modern building services rely. In the 1870s the UK saw the first great public works to increase urban sanitation and the building of reservoirs and underground aqueducts to bring clean water to urban centres like Manchester and Birmingham. During the twentieth century local electrical supplies have grown into a national grid. Gas supplies, which were organized on a local basis until the 1950s, were transformed into a national network after the discovery of North Sea gas. The latest networks are to do with information technology in the form of voice and data transmission.

People in the developed countries now expect high levels of servicing in all buildings, including adequate heating, clean water, disposal of waste products and good levels of lighting.[2] These are seen as the prerequisites for satisfactory living standards and are used as measures in such assessments as the English House Condition Survey. Such levels of servicing require active servicing systems relying on mechanical systems and electrical power to drive them.

However, their very complexity can give rise to problems which in turn influence design innovation. For example, the development of air-conditioning in relation to modern offices has been influenced by the need to remove energy generated by lighting and solar gain, as a result of the fashion for deep floor plans, large window areas and the increasing use of electrical equipment.

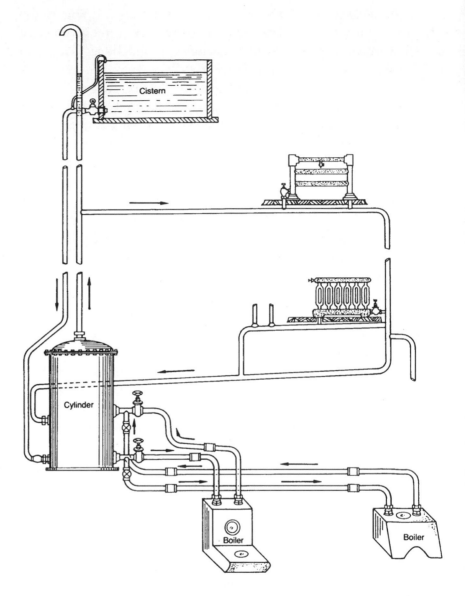

Figure 9.2 Hot-water apparatus with two boilers, cylinder system, *ca.* 1900.

The resultant need to remove large amounts of heat energy has given rise to the development of water-based induction type air-conditioning in place of all-air systems. This is because water is many times more efficient as a heat transfer medium than air, the transfer of energy in all-air systems being impractical because of the requirement for large ducts to circulate the air.[3]

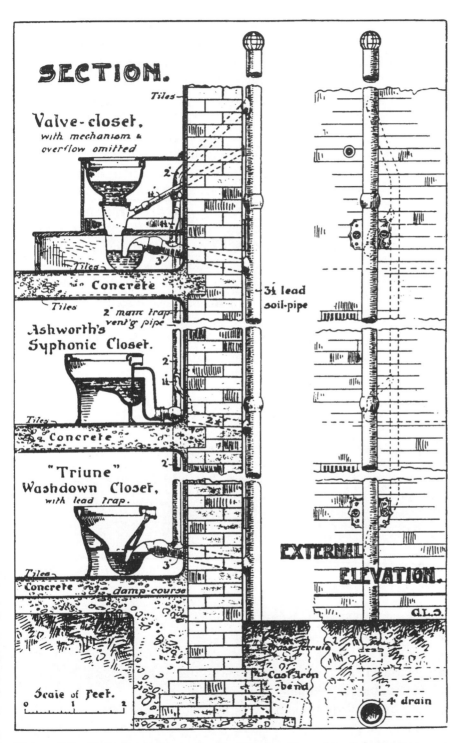

Figure 9.3 Soil-pipe and trap-ventilating pipes for a tier of three closets, *ca.*
1900.

There is an interesting history to the sanitation systems that we currently use. The Victorian obsession with the need to separate the occupants of buildings from air from the foul drain resulted in the 'two pipe system' of drainage. In this system the waste water and the foul water (that containing human excreta) were discharged into two separate vertical stacks. The crowns of all of the traps associated with each appliance were then connected to separate ventilation pipes which were opened to the outside air. It was not until the 1960s that the design of these systems was challenged as a result of extensive research carried out at the Building Research Establishment at Garston. Their findings resulted in a basic understanding of fluid flows in drainage pipes and the perfection of the current single-stack system of drainage. This system gives large cost and space savings whilst still performing adequately.

Active mechanical and electrical building services have come a long way in this century. They can deliver utilities to any part of a building, remove waste materials, transport people, provide sophisticated lighting, closely control the thermal environment and ensure safety in the form of security and fire detection systems and fire fighting installations. Modern living depends upon them.[2]

WORKPIECE 9.1

DEVELOPMENT OF SERVICES

Identify three reasons why the development of services within buildings has not been linear.

Explain why power in the form of electricity has been so important to the development of services.

Give two examples of how electrical power has encouraged or made possible the development of specific services installations.

Why should the lack of skilled labour influence the design of a service system?

SERVICES ENGINEERING SKILLS

A modern multi-storey office building will normally contain the following services systems:

- air-conditioning and ventilation;
- cold water supply;
- hot water supply;
- sanitation in the form of foul and surface water drainage;
- fire detection and fighting systems;
- electrical distribution network for power to drive lighting and machines;
- gas supply;
- lightning protection;

- telecommunications systems for voice and data transmission;
- lifts for rapid vertical circulation.

Because of the variety and complexity of services installations, their design goes beyond the ability of any one engineer. Each service is designed by a specialist consultant who has the ability to produce a services system which meets agreed design criteria and controlling legislation. The coordination of these services within the building must then be undertaken by a specialist architect or a services consultant.

Since a services installation is essentially an assembly of components, there is a comprehensive support industry of manufacturers and suppliers. Each component used has to be designed by scientist/engineers who understand the role of their component in the context of the particular services installation. These component designers are in turn supported by material technology specialists such as metallurgists, industrial chemists and specialist manufacturers.

Because of the chequered history of the operation of building services systems, with many failures especially in respect of fires and explosions, a large body of legislation has been created in the UK and implemented through relevant regulations and codes of practice.[2] Much of this control, aimed at preventing injury, sickness and death as the result of bad design operations, now incorporates European codes. The designer must therefore not only achieve adequate performance of the services installation but also do so within current legislative constraints.

A major consideration which must be taken into account by the designer of an individual service is the relationship between that service and any other service which it might affect. The designers of telecommunication systems must consider the effect of alternating magnetic flux generated by alternating voltage power cables because these may corrupt electrical computing data. Designers of lift installations must liaise with the designers of the electrical installations to insure adequate power supplies. Indeed the relationship between every service and every other service must be considered.

WORKPIECE 9.2

SERVICES COMPLEXITY

Give three reasons why the design of all of the services installations and services components within a large modern building is beyond the ability of any one services engineer.

Find examples of service failures that have caused injury or death and explain what went wrong.

179

THE INTERRELATION-SHIP BETWEEN BUILDING SERVICES AND THE OVERALL BUILDING DESIGN

In a modern highly serviced commercial building over 50% of the total cost of the building will be in respect of services. Both the volume and complexity of building services are increasing. Therefore two problems must be addressed when considering the incorporation of building services in the overall building design:

● the effect of the space requirements of the services on the spatial and structural design of the building;
● the compatibility of the individual services with each other.[4]

Close cooperation between the designers of the services and the building is essential. The circulation of services around the building to the point of delivery is an increasingly complex puzzle. All services in large buildings are contained in horizontal and vertical ducts: coordination of duct design and the individual services in these ducts is best achieved by the appointment of a ductwork supervisor. Services will also need to be maintained and altered during the life of the building and adequate space must be provided in the initial design. The rapid increase in computing technology in modern business practice has led to new service problems in managing the complex cable networks that link computers.

The space requirements for services should be incorporated in the building design from the earliest sketches. If sufficient space is not allowed for in the initial concept, it can be extremely difficult to achieve a satisfactory solution in the completed project.[4] The space allowances at the outline stage can be estimated from existing data and 'rules of thumb'. For example, the size of low velocity air ducts may be determined by dividing the volume flow rate required by $4 \, \mathrm{m \, s^{-1}}$, or vertical ducts for piped or electrical services usually require duct cross sectional areas of $1–2 \, \mathrm{m^2}$ for each $5000 \, \mathrm{m^3}$ building volume. Between 10% and 15% should be added to these areas to allow for future alterations.

There are also certain other overriding guidelines which have been established by experience: ceiling voids should have a minimum depth of 500 metres free of structural members; to avoid excessively deep ceiling voids, vertical ducts should serve a maximum area of $1000 \, \mathrm{m^3}$; raised floors must allow for sufficient access to be able to alter cabling.[4]

In the early stages of the design of a building, it is not feasible to determine the required distribution duct capacity for each of the services separately, therefore a unified or overall approach is needed. By grouping the services installations within a ductwork system or within cores rather than distributing them separately, the following advantages may be gained:

● Installation is simpler.
● Faults are reduced since the major work on each service can be carried out in one operation.
● The requirement that services be accessible for maintenance and repair is met.

The increasing use of services ducts has important structural implications. It is generally sensible to locate openings for ducts where stress in the structure is low and to site vertical ducts adjacent to vertical members. Lateral ducts often conflict with the structure. Sometimes holes can be made in beams or special open lattice beams can be employed to allow the passage of services. Where the conflict cannot be overcome, the solution may be to increase the number of vertical ducts.[2]

One of the most critical problems is not the physical size of the distribution pipes but the necessity for branches to cross the line of other services. Duct sizes are also often dictated by the space required where vertical services branch into horizontal ducts. Duct size ultimately becomes a planning problem but may have a major influence on building height and may affect foundation design strength: it therefore has major cost implications.

Services ducts may be formed as part of the building structure or be non-loadbearing elements. The general fashion is for services to be hidden within buildings and not on view. However, spectacular examples like the Pompidou Centre in Paris and Lloyds Building in London by Richard Rogers have shown that the externalization of services can be used to dramatic architectural effect. Generally services are distributed horizontally and vertically in a building using ducts and a services core. The term 'services core' is applied to a conglomerate of services elements which may be as simple as a kitchen/bathroom unit for a house or as complex as the services elements for a high-rise office block. Common to both is the bringing together of services, mainly for economy. Another benefit gained by the use of service cores is the closeness of piped and ducted services and circulation areas which allow maintenance and control without interfering with main floor areas.

Because of their inherently rigid structural form, vertical services cores are often used to provide lateral stability. When positioned centrally, they may carry a large proportion of the floor loads. This results in the core walls being highly stressed, particularly at the base. The size and positioning of holes in walls must therefore be decided at an early stage and designed for. There will also be areas of structural restriction immediately above and below intersections between the floors and the core walls where the floor loads are carried.

In medium-rise buildings with extended floor plans (like hotels) where piped and ducted services outlets are dispersed, the grouping of these services near vertical circulation may be inappropriate. Instead a series of vertical ducts will be necessary and the services cores will contain only lifts, stairs, main electrical risers, telecomunications and flues.

Service cores are generally located away from the building perimeter in areas not in demand as living or office space, leaving large unobstructed floor spaces.

WORKPIECE 9.3

INCORPORATION OF SERVICES

Identify ways in which space requirements for services are allowed for at the design stage.

Draw a detail of a typical vertical and a horizontal duct.

What problems would you face putting modern ductwork in a Victorian building? How would services have to be modified to fit in?

The fact that service ducts penetrate throughout the building means that they are a potential route for the rapid distribution of lethal hazards, especially fire. Indeed the services themselves are a major potential source for such hazards. Services ducts and their contents must be designed to prevent rapid distribution. When a service duct passes from one compartment to another, fire separation should be maintained by constructing the duct, including access doors, so that it has the same fire resistance characteristics as the fire compartment wall or floor through which it passes.

Services pipes and air-conditioning ducts penetrating a fire-resisting division must be either contained within a fire-resisting duct or protected by a sealing system. For example, small pipes can be sleeved and sealed with a patent flexible mastic or concreted in, and ventilation trunking must incorporate a fire damper.

Unless suitable precautions are taken, services ducts themselves may be a place where fire starts or grows undetected or people become trapped. Adequate fire precautions must therefore be taken to prevent the occurrence of a fire in ducts, detect a fire in its early stages, provide means of escape for occupants and prevent the spread of fire and smoke through the building.

The consequence of the failure of services, either individually or in

FIRE SAFETY

Buildings are often divided into fire compartments. Give reasons why the penetration of fire compartment walls by services conduits may pose a threat to the safety of the contents of a building or its occupants.

In your answer, illustrate two examples of how fire spread is prevented at the point where conduits pass through a fire compartment wall.

conjunction with other services, must be considered. If this could induce a hazard either to the services or to personnel, then the services should be segregated. For example, water and other fluids can cause damage by corrosion and solvent action or by lowering electrical resistance. Hot fluids can cause damage by overheating and a jet of fluid escaping from a pressurized service pipe can cause damage by force of impact. The contents of some pipes may be poisonous or infectious.[2]

A good example of the safety of services and their possible interaction is given in the case of telecommunication and power cables. Here there are two aspects to be considered: safety and interference.

ELECTRICAL SAFETY

Telecommunications cables have in the past been distributed within electrical risers. It is strongly recommended that, for new buildings, they be contained within a separate vertical duct. This duct will of course contain all associated power supplies for telecommunication needs and be installed in accordance with the Institute of Electrical Engineers Wiring Regulations. When telecommunication cables are located within an existing electrical duct and in common with electrical power cables, careful consideration must be given to the relationship between telecommunication cables and all power cables in that duct. The two sets of cables must be separated by a specified distance or a physical insulating barrier and where cables cross they must be separated by an insulating bridge. Under no circumstances should power and telecommunication cables share the same conduit or enclosing trunking.

ELECTRICAL INTERFERENCE

Interference and damage may be caused by electromagnetic induction. Electrical power cables generate an alternating magnetic field which can induce voltages into adjacent cables. These induced voltages may be of the same order of magnitude as the power cable's supply. Such induced voltages may be dangerous and/or damage telecommunications equipment. It is recommended that power cables be separated by a solid barrier from telecommunication cables or separated by a space of not less than 100 mm.

THE CONTRIBUTION OF SERVICES TO THE QUALITY ENVIRONMENT

As suggested in the introduction to this chapter, a quality environment is one which is safe, comfortable and convenient. Active services have made a substantial contribution to the provision of a quality environment, working as they do in conjunction with the fabric of the building. They respond to the external climate and provide an internal environment which is conducive to the use of the building.

Building services make possible the provision of a quality environment within buildings which could not be provided solely by passive means. In this respect, therefore, it is the inclusion of sophisticated services installations in the modern buildings which makes them so fundamentally different in design to that of traditional buildings. The growth of the internal environment can be categorized under the headings of safety, comfort and convenience.[5]

SAFETY

The quality environment must by definition be one in which an individual is physically safe. For example, the provision of artificial lighting throughout the modern building may be taken for granted, but without it the building environment would be very dangerous. Water supplies within the building which are free from contamination are essential to the good health of the occupants. Fire safety within buildings nowadays relies heavily upon the incorporation of automatic fire detection and alarm systems, emergency lighting and fire extinguishing systems.

COMFORT

The contribution made by building services installations to the comfort of the individual can be broken down into three main areas: thermal, acoustic and visual.

Building services installations are the means by which the internal climate is controlled in the context of the overall building thermal performance. The supply and removal of heat energy and the modification of the quality of air within the building are the province of the appropriate services installation such as the heating system, mechanical ventilation or air-conditioning systems.

The acoustic environment may be modified actively using background masking sound or active electronic sound-deadening measures to control low frequency sound from ducts.

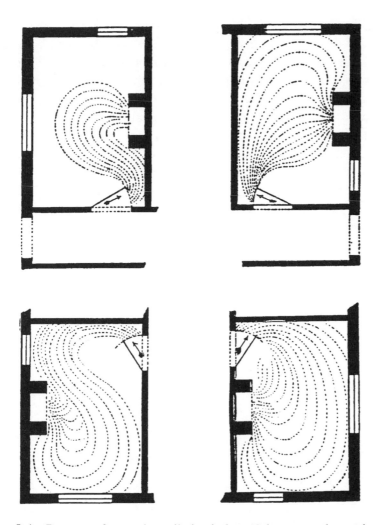

Figure 9.4 Patterns of natural ventilation in late 19th century domestic rooms.

The passive visual environment may be enhanced by lighting systems which may be used to create atmosphere or improve the ease with which visual tasks may be carried out.

A quality environment in the case of a building must be one where people are able to function at their best. This means that their immediate physical needs must be met, and every facility provided for their comfort and efficiency.

Developments ranging from modern sanitary systems, lifts and telecommunication systems have raised standards and therefore the expectations of the occupants of buildings. In a modern hotel, for

CONVENIENCE

185

example, patrons expect to find their room serviced with electrical power and lighting systems; telecommunication, data and video links; and en suite sanitary accommodation which includes unlimited supplies of cold and hot running water and sanitary conveniences. All of these systems are part of a complex infrastructure of services systems.

There is no doubt that the key to the function of most, if not all, services installations required within buildings is the provision of adequate supplies of electrical power. It is electricity in the form of micro electronics which is currently having the greatest effect upon development and innovation in building services, both in the form of a solution to services problems and in the placing of demands upon them.[1]

However, such is the complexity of servicing problems that we do not always get it right. Much research is currently being carried out into sick building syndrome [6] whereby office workers in air-conditioned offices have constant low-grade infections. This is thought to be caused by imbalances within air-conditioning systems. Similarly, legionnaires' disease is caused by poor maintenance practices on air-conditioning filters.[5]

WORKPIECE 9.5

QUALITY ENVIRONMENT – SERVICES CONTRIBUTION

Explain, giving examples, the term 'quality environment'. Is your working environment a 'quality' environment?
Why is it that building services systems are becoming more and more sophisticated and complicated?
What factors are likely to be responsible for sick building syndrome?

SUMMARY

This chapter has shown that, although sophisticated building services are by no means a modern phenomenon, the growth of electrical and mechanical services in buildings, supported by a national infrastructure of service distribution, has been rapid and sustained since the Industrial Revolution. Electrical power has played a particularly important part in this development.

People today expect a high level of comfort, convenience and safety within buildings which can only be supplied and sustained by active service installations. These are both expensive to provide and expensive to run. The development of building services continues to be rapid and the likelihood that services may have to be adapted and altered several times within the life of a building poses major problems for those who manage buildings.

Services are a potential source of hazards within buildings and service engineers must ensure that services are safely contained within ducts and that incompatible services are separated. In this respect engineers must comply with the heavy burden of national and European legislation. They must also ensure that service installations can be maintained and adapted easily and safely. The service engineer is therefore an important part of both the design team and the maintenance team.

Active services have made possible a high quality internal environment for most people in the UK and have raised our expectations of what is acceptable as an internal environment. It has made living in high rise buildings and working with modern information technology possible. However, we do not always get it right and sick building syndrome and legionnaires' disease are a reminder of the complexity of building services problems and the need for continued development.

KEY CONCEPTS

- Some ancient buildings had sophisticated but non-mechanical services.
- Modern services are mechanical and require energy to run them.
- Mechanical and electrical services have proliferated since the Industrial Revolution.
- Modern buildings can be completely sealed from external climate but increase the risk of ill health if the active systems do not work properly.
- Service design must be closely coordinated with the overall building design.
- Service design must allow for maintenance and alteration.
- Services are a potential source of hazards and must be protected.
- Service engineers require high levels of design and coordination skills.

REFERENCES

1. Mumford, L. (1987) *The City in History*, Penguin.
2. Burberry, P. (1992) *Environment and Services*, 7th edn, Batsford.
3. Hall, F. (1987) *Building Services and Equipment*, Vols 1 and 2, Longman.
4. 'Space for Services' series, *Architects Journal*, 12 Feb–26 March 1986.
5. Holdsworth, W. and Sealey, A.F (1992) *Healthy Buildings*, Longman.
6. Bradshaw, V. (1993) *Building Control Systems*, 2nd edn, BWL.

FURTHER READING

Barton, P.K. (1983) *Building Services Integration*, E & FN Spon.

BS 8313 1898, *Accommodation of services in ducts*.

Building Regulations.

Chadderton, D.V. (1991) *Building Services Engineering*, E & FN Spon.

Chadderton, D.V. (1993) *Air-conditioning – A Practical Guide*, E & FN Spon.

CIBSE Guide.

Designing against Fire. *Building Services Journal*, Sept. 1981.

Eastop, J.D. and Watson, W.E. (1992) *Mechanical Services for Buildings*, Longman.

IEE Regulations, 16th edn.

Shields, T.D and Silcock, G.H.H. (1987) *Buildings on Fire*, Longmans.

Woolley, L. (1990) *Sanitation Details*, E & FN Spon.

Woolley, L. (1988) *Drainage Details*, E & FN Spon.

INDIVIDUAL AND COLLECTIVE RESPONSIBILITIES

TONY COLLIER

CHAPTER TEN

10

What kind of changes do we face today? How will these affect the way we work?

THEME

In the late 1980s and early 1990s the world saw political, economic, social and technical changes on an unprecedented scale. Previously unimaginable shifts of power took place, for example in Europe with the demolition of the Berlin Wall. Civil war raged in Yugoslavia but the Middle East came closer to a long-term peace settlement than it has ever been before.

Tragedy struck the African continent which has suffered one of the worst famines there has ever been. In Rwanda, civil war caused massive population movements. The western world has been faced with a severe recession and even Japan has seen its economy dented. In Russia inflation ran at well over 100% p.a. in 1994. In the Far East, Hong Kong prepared to be handed to the Chinese.

This is the context in which we work. In this chapter we shall be reflecting on the challenges that we have identified in the rest of the book and shall try to understand these implications in a world of change.

Figure 10.1 Checkpoint Charlie in Berlin (now demolished). (Tom Muir.)

OBJECTIVES

By the end of the chapter you should be able to:

● analyse the changing context in which we live;

● understand the range of skills, expertise and thinking that a professional needs to employ;

● understand the need for the individual to be able to work on their own as well as in a group context;

● assess your own priorities for operating in a rapidly changing world.

INTRODUCTION

As individuals in society, we have to be able to make value judgements and decisions which affect our own and other people's lives. Much of professional education reflects the preoccupations of the individual professions rather than the nature and context of the world in which we work and the values we have to confront and weigh up in our lives. To some extent this is inevitable, given the way that the professions have evolved and the pattern of life in the twentieth century. All professional bodies have professional codes of conduct, the origins of which placed a significant emphasis on ethical issues concerned with the service they offered to society. With the increasing polarization of groups within society, there is a need to address the way professions operate and the education and training provided for, and by, them. These issues are addressed in Book 1 (*Collaborative Practice in the Built Environment*), which focuses on the professional context and the nature of working together in collaborative interdisciplinary groups. However, these are also questions which are important in the context of this book.

As professionals we need to be able to understand the nature of the design and development process and integrate the role of technology within it. This is the very core of our activity. Because of the polarization of groups within society, this is too often forgotten. As a result planners, architects, surveyors and engineers (and I use these terms generally to cover all the built environment professions) as well as funders, politicians, clients and users often spend more time jockeying for influence (to demonstrate that their own roles and influence are more important than anyone else's) than they do working together to create an efficient, effective quality service – hence quality environment. The reasons for this are complex and include:

- the structure and organization of the professions and industry;
- polarization of groups within society;
- the way professional values are inculcated at an early stage;
- the appeal of the professions to a particular group of young people looking for status and security;
- inflexible and narrow education and training.

In this book we have identified and discussed key ingredients in the development process. We have identified issues concerning design and technology, the impact of technology on society and the nature of social change. This has ranged from the mass movement of people to the challenge of science and new inventions and the creation of new designs. For each generation, there is not only the past to understand and present problems to solve but also unpredictable new changes. As a result, professionals have to be able to cope with the unforeseen in addition to the well known. This is why value judgements and decision-making are so important. Assessing solutions, weighing up evidence and coming to decisions, whether they are about the way we are working or how we detail the junctions between the wall and the roof of a building, have important implications and are the result of assessing evidence.

Figure 10.2 New structures, new materials: Munich Olympic Stadium, designed by Frei Otto. (Tom Muir.)

CHANGES IN DESIGN

During the 1980s the dominant style of architecture – 'modernism' or the 'international style' – was increasingly the subject of criticism and hostility. In the UK this is most easily signified by the attack on modern architects made by HRH Prince Charles at a speech at Hampton Court in 1984. But this attack was only a symbol of widespread concern about the scale and thoughtlessness of much modern development. In the USA, radical new design movements were occuring as the growth of post-modernism took place. This was reflected in Europe and across the world. By the late 1980s the number of viable styles and approaches to design had increased dramatically – classicism and deconstructivism being just two of them. Along with this diversification, organizations and movements like Community Architecture, Community Technical Aid and Planning Aid evolved. Young professionals involved in these new movements saw themselves as working with local people for the common good, assisting communities in realizing their ideas rather than having the ideas of others thrust on them.

In the 1990s it is therefore not only the international political and economic backdrop that is changing but also the nature and operation of the professions. Furthermore, technology is changing as well.

In the 1980s computers were just being introduced into education and practice. In the 1990s enormous advances are being made in the size, specification and cost of hardware. New software is transforming the potential performance of anyone who is computer literate. Virtual reality systems are being introduced in the world of entertainment while medical research is radically changing with advances in neurosurgery and in the use of new information systems. Computers are being used to assist in the operation and management of buildings. The first generation of 'intelligent' buildings is emerging as increasingly sophisticated hardware and software is introduced into the building fabric.

In Japan, which invests a far higher proportion of income in research, considerable emphasis is being placed on robotics and the development of new automated technology which will operate on site in the construction of buildings.[1]

Integral to all this is the rapid advance in electronics and the creation of the 'global information highway'. Information Technology promises to swamp us all in an onslaught of new digital developments.

It is interesting to note that in George Orwell's novel *1984*, 'the impact of Big Brother' as a form of state control was widely feared. Yet in 1994 the citizens of towns and cities are welcoming television surveillance of shopping centres, public places and housing estates as part of a wide effort to curb crime. Where should the influence of 'Big Brother' stop and personal security begin?

New lightweight structures, energy efficient materials, experimental building methods and new building procurement methods are just some of the technical developments that professionals have to accommodate in their tendering.

The growth of new methods of providing buildings, the possibility of widely fluctuating interest rates, and shifts in financial policies which combine private with public money are all making an impact on the industry. New markets are opening up – in the European community, in Eastern Europe and Russia. The Pacific rim is increasingly seen to be the focus for the global economy.

How should we react to these changes? What impact will they have on UK industry in the next millennium? What can we do now to prepare ourselves for further radical changes in society? Are there constants in this world of change?

WORKPIECE 10.1

TECHNOLOGICAL CHANGE

Identify the three most important technological changes in the past 25 years.

How have these affected building design?

What technological changes do you believe will influence designs in the next 25 years and how?

THE POSITION OF THE UK CONSTRUCTION AND DEVELOPMENT INDUSTRY IN THE ECONOMY

Over the past 20 years the structure of the industry has changed dramatically. It has become increasingly fragmented between very small and very large businesses. In the UK there are over 200 000 contracting businesses, of which 45% are one-person firms and only 12% employ more than seven people. Large construction businesses (employing 80 persons or more) accounted for over 40% of the £43.3 billion worth of business transacted in 1993, which itself represented 8% of Gross Domestic Product. Thus the industry makes a significant contribution to the economy. The fragmentation into a large number of very small businesses and a small number of large firms which account for a significant share of the work creates major problems of planning, coordination, research and innovation, all of which bear directly upon design, technology and the development process.

The industry is a major component of the national economy in all the developed countries. The impact of construction industry projects on the economy in terms of jobs, trade and development is substantial. How governments steer their economies and their view of the construction industry as an indicator is fundamentally important to anyone working in the built environment professions.

Increased public expenditure in the infrastructure increases job prospects in the industry. For example, if a government decides to invest more in (public) housing, schools or any other sector, it will brighten the industry's prospects. But what leads governments into policy making like this? How can (or should) the professions influence government? How do policy changes like these affect tomorrow's young professional? How should we react as students and professionals?

Part of our job is to ensure that at any stage of our personal development we are up-to-date. No one can contribute to a team if they lack practical reliable skills. Wherever we operate we need to be able to perform everyday tasks and satisfy the operational needs of clients.

This is not enough by itself. We also need to be flexible, analytical and creative both as individuals and in teams. As professionals we need to be able to identify new and emerging problems, hypothesize about them and find solutions to them. Unless we can respond to change in a positive and imaginative way, using our creative powers to invent solutions to new problems, we will be swamped.

Traditionally there has been a tendency for the design professions in the built environment to look on themselves as problem solvers while the non-design professions provide the contextual reference points. This is no longer true. All built environment professionals have to be problem solvers – albeit of varying kinds. Design of course plays a critical role in the manipulation and creation of space, form, materials and technology to solve complex (and simple) building problems that people can understand and enjoy. But the major challenges are now so complex that more collective approaches to problem solving are essential, with the designer understanding the nature of the wider context and clearly operating within it.

All built environment professionals need to be aware of the linkages between them, the nature of team work and the relationship between the various parts of the whole design, development and construction process.[2] It is of little use for architects to dream up endless schemes that are neither economically viable, technically feasible nor socially relevant. This does not mean there is no role for the idiosyncratic individual or for people to challenge the nature and organization of society or the professions through new and inventive ideas and design (indeed it is very necessary that they do). It does, however, require a change in attitude among many educationists and professionals about the way we work.[3, 4]

Now that you are reaching the end of this book you will understand how vital it is, not only to be critically aware of your own field, but also to understand the complexity and interrelationship between design, technology and the development process. You may be interested to know that there have been few, if any, attempts until this book to write about the nature of the whole process rather than just one bit of it. Until now almost all the textbooks have been written from a very specific viewpoint – normally by one professional writing primarily from their own perspective, although of course sometimes this has led to publications of wider interest.

In this final chapter we therefore wish to do five things:

● Highlight education and training needs (personal and professional) in a changing world.

THE INTEGRATION OF DESIGN, TECHNOLOGY AND THE DEVELOPMENT PROCESS

- Refer to the wider issues concerned in the BEST series.
- Bring together the various strands of this book.
- Explore through detailed examination some of the issues we have covered.
- Reflect on the nature of change and its future impact on society and the professions.

Historically the development and construction industries in the UK are considered to be fragmented and divisive. Although you may not be aware of it, this is a major issue for students today as the changes that are now being discussed about how the professions operate will have a major impact when they come into force.

The fragmentation and divisions within the industry have been a concern of government and groups like the National Property Federation and National Contractor's Group for some time. An industry which is split into many separate bodies results in inefficient practices, for example where professionals spend too much time jockeying for position and taking up confrontational positions with each other, rather than getting down to sorting things out together.[4]

Attempts have been made to bring the industry together through, for example, the Construction Industry Council, various conferences, the former National Economic Development Office, the Construction Industry Standing Conference and others. The structure and organization of the construction industry is of fundamental importance to any government.

One of the shifts that has occured in the UK as a result of these processes and changes is the move towards more integrated education and training whereby all professions are encouraged to work together. These books are a direct result of this movement and are stimulated by the pioneering educational development which has taken place in the Faculty of the Built Environment at the University of Central England. This work has involved major studies of what is taught on courses and a reorganization of courses so that young professionals studying for their first professional qualifications actually learn together for around 20% of their time.[3]

INTERNATIONAL COMPARISONS

In the UK the industry and professions have been organized on very traditional lines with a clear demarcation between each player. This is not so true in Germany, Japan or the USA where there has been a more integrated approach to the industry and the professions for some time.

Japan is a good example of a country where the construction industry is organized into a more cohesive system and which has become a world leader in this field. Since the second world war, Japanese construction firms have gained major footholds in the international construction market. The rate of growth in the international market during the period 1970–1985 was phenomenal with overseas construction activities rising from around half a billion dollars in 1973 to nearly seven billion dollars (including subsidiaries) in 1985.[5]

How has this happened? What changes can be made in the UK industry to improve its rating once again? How can the Japanese maintain their position? How do Germany and the USA compare?

WORKPIECE 10.2

POST-WAR PROJECTS

Identify the three most important post-war construction projects in your area (e.g. building a ring road, major housing estate, demolishing an important listed building etc).
Identify/explore the following for each example:

● The political context at the time the decision was taken, including the key players responsible for the decision.
● Public reaction at the time the decision was taken and public reaction now to the results of the decision.

● The nature of the professional team which implemented the decision, e.g. which professional led the team, what professions were represented on the team.

Evaluate whether or not you feel that those involved in the project took the right decision and obtained 'quality results'.
Discuss how you would now go about this project identifying where you would make different decisions and why.

Some of these issues are explored in Book 1 while the management and business techniques necessary to ensure that the appropriate services are provided and used are covered in Book 3 (*Management and Business Skills for the Built Environment*). However, it is also worth noting that despite the problems faced by UK industry as a whole, the UK has generated more internationally well known and respected designers than any other country in the world. Sir Norman Foster, Sir Richard Rogers and the late James Stirling haved achieved major international acclaim. Can the distinctiveness of UK designers be sustained if the nature and organization of the industry changes along with the provision of education and training needed to support the industry?

QUALITY

Whatever contribution we make, there is one issue that transcends all others and that is quality. Whether we aspire to be architects, planners, surveyors, builders, engineers or landscape architects, we are all ultimately concerned with promoting the quality of the built environment.

At each stage of the design, development and construction process there are different foci to emphasize. Early stages of a project may be more concerned with the assembly of land, the definition of new social issues or the provision of funding. Later stages will emphasize the design and technological sides. While many projects are carried out in a predictable process, it must also be recognized that buildings and developments can also come about for entirely different reasons. A classic example of a popular and highly visited place that defies all the usual logic (and would almost certainly be impossible to build today) is Portmeirion – the Ravenna of North Wales. This italianate village was built by Clough Williams-Ellis, a highly idiosyncratic architect, who travelled the world before finding his ideal site in Wales. The village was built in Clough's lifetime using local labour to his own personal designs, financed, managed and organized by himself. The implementation of such a dream would not pass today's planning control. Indeed because the village is now a conservation area it is itself controlled by planning legislation. The owners have great difficulty in changing their own creation!

Nevertheless, despite its idiosyncrasy, Clough Williams-Ellis him-

Figure 10.3 Portmeirion, a romantic personal vision designed and built by Clough Williams-Ellis. (Richard Andrews.)

self had to undertake in his own way all the processes we have discussed in this book. In many respects it is easier to sum up the process as a whole by discussing Clough's creation in detail than it is to explain a more typical current building project. As the architect, owner, developer and builder, Clough Williams-Ellis needed to understand the nature of the materials available to him and the availability of local labour. He was steeped in his own understanding of the past and was deeply knowledgeable about the history of architecture in so far as it related to his philosophy. He had to raise the finance and, of course, make the place 'pay' and be popular at the end. Quality and design were paramount in his thinking.[6]

Other equally characteristic examples exist. Frank Lloyd Wright, one of the greatest twentieth century architects, twice set out to realize his dreams in places that he owned, funded, created and made work. One was Taliesin East in Wisconsin, USA, and the other Taliesin West near Phoenix, Arizona.

One of the pupils at Taliesin West was Paolo Solieri. He set up in turn another centre, in many ways more experimental, known as Arcosanti. This extraordinary place is built out of earth-moulded concrete and was financed largely by Solieri making bells, for which he

Figure 10.4 Acrosanti: central space designed and built by Paolo Soleri using earth-moulded concrete. Viewed through line of bells. (Tony Collier.)

became famous and sold throughout the world including to the Vatican. But again, despite everything being concentrated into one man's creative vision and brought about by extraordinary passion, the nature of what was created still reflects the processes that we have discussed in this book. Indeed the coming together of the whole process in one person and one team underlines the need for an integrated approach to design, technology and the development processes even more.

Figure 10.5 Taliesian West, Frank Lloyd Wright's centre; now the home of Frank Lloyd Wright Foundation. (Tony Collier.)

Vision – whether it is individual or a collective shared vision – is the key force. These three examples emphasize the importance of vision and creativity in the design and development process. Other examples would include William Morris, the Victorian writer, designer and visionary politician. In assessing the importance of people like Morris, critics have until recently tended to focus on his writing and designs. However, Morris was a successful businessman who ran a thriving commercial concern. This side of him is just as important.

Provided that the individual can sustain a high level of decision-making and achieve their desired vision and ideas, the approach of people like Williams-Ellis, Wright and Solieri can lead to remarkable results, as has been shown. The vast majority of projects, however, are much more complex, requiring contributions from a wide range of people. The activities of one or two individuals within this may still dominate the thinking behind, and resulting quality of, a development project. However, with a team involved and a project being subject to all the usual processes of planning and building regulations approval, satisfying client and funding needs as well as user requirements and public taste, the process is complex.

So how do we promote quality design in more complex situations? How can built environment professionals work with the client, local government councillors who sit on planning committees, local authority officers and others to establish a climate in which a quality environment – good design – will flourish?

In Birmingham, England, there has been an innovative development that has brought people together from all walks of life to discuss and promote quality design. The scheme is known as the Birmingham Design Initiative and has been formulated and organized by a mixed group of multi-disciplinary professionals, local councillors and officers and representatives of education, business, industry and the community. The scheme was first launched when the City of Birmingham Council was setting out its own agenda for re-establishing Birmingham as a major international city. The quality of design was felt to be a vital ingredient in this programme. Initially the group (then known as the Good Design Initiative) created an experimental 2-year programme of seminars, workshops, think-tanks, lectures, international competitions and conferences. The programme attracted major sponsorship and offered attractive events and activities for the local community as well as people from other countries. The International Design Conference attracted delegates and speakers from the UK and abroad. The International Design Competition attracted multi-disciplinary team entries from nearly 30 different countries. The purpose of the competition was to generate new ideas and designs for inner city sites. The board of assessors included distinguished international designers as well as local councillors and representatives of the professions. The theme throughout was working together, but behind this there was a clear vision about quality and design. The initiative has since gone on to launch and run activities including proposals for a major new Design Centre celebrating the diversity of design and manufacturing in the city.

Finance for running this programme has come from a variety of

PROMOTING DESIGN

sources. First the Steering Group (or committee) has given its time voluntarily. This means that a large number of distinguished local people are actively contributing their time free of charge. This draws in other support and enables the group to influence all sorts of other people. Secondly the group attracts sponsorship. So far it has raised well over £100 000 in cash (much more including contributions in kind). This has helped fund prizes for the competition, administration and other activities, although much of the administration is done voluntarily. Thirdly, institutions who support the scheme generously provide assistance; for example, the University of Central England and the City of Birmingham Council both provide administrative support. Further, the initiative has a group of members who each pay in small subscriptions to help to fund the programme. This combination of help in kind, sponsorship and administrative assistance has been a powerful ingredient in the successful implementation of the scheme. In 1993, about four years after the project was launched, the *Birmingham Post* (the main local newspaper) ran a feature praising the success of the initiative in helping Birmingham regain its image as a City of Quality. The role of the media is very important in a programme like this.

This kind of approach has been developed elsewhere in the UK and in Europe and the USA. Forming partnerships to promote understanding about the realization of good design is vital for the future of towns and cities everywhere. As students you need to develop these skills and approaches now so that you will be able to play as creative a role as possible when you qualify.

Design is a key ingredient in the creation of a quality environment, but all the team plays its part in establishing the context and process in which good design flourishes. Designers are not the only ones who can have ideas about buildings and places, but they are of course expected to have a high level of skill and imagination in the creative design process.

If we cast our minds back to earlier chapters, we can recall how technology has impacted on society and the environment, how social movements influence and set the context for the creation of new buildings and places and how, despite centuries of evolution and the innovations of widely different styles of building and design, there are still fundamental similarities between buildings of different ages and types.

CHANGES IN HEALTH CENTRES

In Chapter 2 we briefly discussed the development of health centres in the context of changing legislation and social needs. In order to cope with the ever changing complexity of the modern world, we need to understand the nature of change. If we take the example of a doctor's group practice surgery, we can further emphasize the nature of the process and the integration of technology within it.

To start with we should consider the political context for a doctor's surgery. This has changed dramatically in the UK in recent years and may well be changing in other parts of the world.

In the UK the changed context results from the new way medical services are financed. Doctors have been encouraged or required to take more control over funding. This has implications not only for the financing of new surgeries but also for the provision of rooms within it. In the early 1980s surgeries were financed on what was then referred to as the 'cost rent scheme' whereby doctors were funded on a beneficial basis on a cost formula relating to the size of the practice and the requirements that the Health Service considered essential. The principles for the funding and provision of accommodation were laid down in a document for all doctors. In the late 1980s the funding arrangements changed. Fewer funds were available for surgeries and so fewer were built. Also, with doctors controlling the funding of their surgery space, an additional 'fund holding' room was added to the accommodation schedule. In the early 1990s, with the growth in National Health Trusts and further restrictions in spending, doctors and their funders are looking for interesting new ways of providing doctors' accommodation. Funders are now looking for developers to include a surgery in a larger scheme. In such a scheme, medical facilities might form the core of a commercial development with the medical centre being rented to the doctors rather than built for them. These changes affect the design team as well as the doctors.

Technology is changing as well. Experiments using sophisticated new technology are being tested and explored. Some of these experiments link local doctors to their nearest hospital with the use of computers and other audiovisual aids. This enables the local doctor to examine a patient, transmitting information to the hospital while the examination takes place so that more specialist advice which may only be available at the hospital can be utilized straight away.

The professional team has to cope with all these changes as well as foresee future needs, all within very tight financial constraints. The changes that are occurring in the provision of doctors' surgeries are a microcosm of the changes occuring in society. No one can foresee the scale and nature of future change. All we do know is that, as professionals, we have to adapt to new demands and assume that we can maintain an effective service within whatever constraints exist at any time.

We could apply the same analysis to changes in the provision of housing or the funding of education in the UK. Parallel changes have occured throughout the world. The former Soviet block is grappling with the introduction of a market economy while the USA is moving towards a new health care system.

WORKPIECE 10.3

IMPORTANT CHANGES

List what you believe to be the most important changes taking place now which will most influence us in the year 2000 under each of the following headings:

- International social trends, e.g. major movements of people, global recession/boom etc.
- International technological trends, e.g. space travel, pollution.
- Regional social trends, e.g. closure of local industry and resultant high levels of unemployment.
- Regional technological trends, e.g. impact of information technology on local services.

Discuss the potential impact of these on you as a professional in 10 years' time under the following headings:

- threats
- opportunities.

Discuss the potential impact of these on the quality of the environment and the visual appearance of buildings, in particular the way buildings in your area will look (existing buildings and new buildings).

THE ROLE OF THE INDIVIDUAL

The key issue is that change is paramount and that all of us have to operate as individuals and professionals in a constantly changing world. As individuals our responsibilities are first and foremost to society as a whole. In this context we then operate as professionals. The role of the individual and the ability of the individual to contribute to common goals and the good of society are of paramount importance. We depend on each other.

The theme we have focused on is at the very core of built environment professional's concerns. However, to achieve quality results, professionals have to be conversant with a number of skills and techniques which are common to all professionals as well as be able to develop their own specialisms to a high level. This book should therefore be read in conjunction with two other core books in the BEST series: *Collaborative Practice in the Built Environment* (Book 1) and *Management and Business Skills for the Built Environment* (Book 3).

The first of these explains the changing nature of the professions and how they operate, with examples of a wide range of projects, buildings, places and skills that professionals are increasingly required to deal with. Book 3 is about the management, business and personal skills that are required for professionals to operate effectively. These books are essential reading for any student studying a built environment course. The three books together cover the material the authors believe should be understood by everyone involved in the built environment.

Subsequent books are planned. They will focus on more specialist subjects which will be of interest to a wide cross section of students.

WORKPIECE 10.4

IMPORTANT GENERATORS

Reflecting back over this book, undertake the following:

1. List the three most important generators of the design and development process.
2. Identify two buildings you know which best illustrate the integration of design, technology and the development process.

Discuss the impact of (1) above on each of the buildings identified in (2) above.

Are there other generators/influences that this book has omitted? What are they? How do they fit in?

Prioritize the five most important generators as you see them now and in 5 years' time.

Which aspect of the creative process are you most interested in: design, technology or the development process? And why? Which is the most important for society?

SUMMARY

In this chapter we have drawn together the strands of the book and emphasized the need for understanding and coming to terms with a rapidly changing world. We have underlined the nature of the design and development process and the integration of technology within it as one of the most fundamental of all human concerns and the core of what built environment professionals do.

The chapter has explored the role of the individual in society and the need to be able to contribute to a collective way of life. We have questioned the organization of professionals and relationships between them; we have looked at their role in the development and construction industry and identified some of the pressures on the professions to change. In this context we have placed the greatest importance on the ability of the professional not only to have the skills and expertise to solve today's problems but also to be able to understand the past and, most importantly, be flexible and adapt to future needs. The ability to analyse new problems and find solutions to them is essential. All professionals play their part in the development process as a whole and should be able to operate as individuals and in teams to foster a worthwhile quality environment that people can understand and enjoy. The ability to create, share and implement a vision is of paramount importance.

KEY CONCEPTS

- All individuals have an important role to play and responsibilities to undertake in society.
- As the professions have evolved, so has society become more polarized. Professional codes of conduct are important but sometimes underused.
- The world is changing very fast; people need to be able to cope with change.
- As professionals we need skills and expertise as well as the ability to be flexible and to be able to perceive new problems and solve them.
- Major changes have occurred in the last ten years and will take place in the next ten. We cannot predict accurately what they will be.
- Design is a key ingredient in the quality of the environment and the way buildings work, but design can be superficial. The availability of finance, government controls and the importance of technology are important.
- The UK professions and building industry are divisive and fragmented. Efforts are being made to change this, including the writing of this book.
- Design, technology and the development process are at the heart of the services provided by built environment professions and at the very core of human endeavour.
- The process of creating the built environment is both an individual and a collective effort. We have as much need to learn from idiosyncractic developments like Portmeirion as we do from major projects like new towns and cities.

REFERENCES

1. Levy, S.M. (1990) *Japanese Construction, An American Perspective*, Van Nostrand Rheinhold.
2. Latham, Sir Michael (1994) *Constructing the Team*, HMSO.
3. Collier, A., Bacon, J., Burns, D. and Muir, T. (1991) *Interdisciplinary Studies in the Built Environment*, Council for National Academic Awards.
4. Darbyshire, Sir Andrew, and Andrews, J. (1993) *Crossing Boundaries*, CIC.
5. Bennett, J., Flanagan, R. and Norman, G. (1987) Capital and Countries Report: the Japanese Construction Industry Centre for Strategic Studies in Construction, University of Reading.
6. Williams-Ellis, Clough (1973) *Portmeirion: The Place and its meaning*, Portmeirion Ltd.

HRH The Prince of Wales (1984) *A Vision of Britain – a view of Architecture*, Doubleday.

Hackney, R. (1990) *The Good, The Bad and the Ugly*, Century Hutchinson Ltd.

Harvey, C. and Press, J. (1993) *William Morris, Design and Enterprise in Victorian Britain*, Manchester University Press.

National Contractors Group (1991) *Building Towards 2001*, Reading University.

RIBA Code of Conduct, RIBA Publications.

INDEX

Also available from E & FN Spon

Brain Train
Studying for success
R. Palmer and S. Pope

The Buildings Around Us
T. Gorst

Construction Contracts
Law and management
J. Murdoch and W. Hughes

Construction Methods and Planning
J.R. Illingworth

Economics
A foundation course for the built environment
J. Manser

Effective Writing
Improving scientific, technical and business communication
C. Turk and J. Kirkman

The Idea of Building
Thought and action in the design and production of buildings
S. Groàk

Project Management Demystified
Today's tools and techniques
G. Reiss

Property Development
D. Cadman and L. Austin-Crowe

Value Management in Design and Construction
J. Kelly and S. Male

For more information, please contact: *The Promotions Department, E & FN Spon,*
2−6 Boundary Row, London SE1 8HN   Tel: 071 865 0066